Fly to Cloud

Prathap Nagarajan
AnandKumar Palanisamy
Venkatanaga Suryanarayana
Archana Raghu
Vimal Manimozhi

DOYENSYS
Technology Drives, We Lead

notionpress
.com

INDIA · SINGAPORE · MALAYSIA

Notion Press

Old No. 38, New No. 6
McNichols Road, Chetpet
Chennai - 600 031

First Published by Notion Press 2019
Copyright © Doyensys 2019
All Rights Reserved.

ISBN 978-1-64760-810-1

CONTENTS

CONTENTS

WHY TO CLOUD

1.1 INTRODUCTION TO FUSION APPLICATIONS - BUILT ON BEST

The Oracle Fusion service-oriented platform and applications suite joins next-generation enterprise technologies, applications, and services, including Oracle Fusion Applications and Oracle Fusion Middleware, to change the dynamics in the applications marketplace and revolutionize business. This chapter provides an introduction to the architecture and components of Oracle Fusion Applications. Using the latest technology and incorporating the best practices gathered from Oracle's customers, Oracle Fusion Applications is a suite of 100% open standards-based business applications that provide a new standard for the way businesses innovate, work and adopt the technology. Delivered as a complete suite of modular, service-enabled enterprise applications, Oracle Fusion Applications works with Oracle's Applications Unlimited portfolio to evolve the business to a new level of performance. Whether it is one module, a product family, or the entire suite, Oracle provides businesses with their choice of all advancements pioneered by Oracle Fusion Applications, at a pace that matches individual business demands.

The Fusion application is built on the best not only on the technology front but also on the functionality derived from the best available ERP in the market. The financial is from Oracle EBS, Human Capital management is from People Soft, Order management is from JD Edwards and CRM from Siebel.

1.2 WHY TO ORACLE CLOUD

The Complete Business platform

Oracle Cloud is built for your entire business, with applications that you can consume as your business grows. With Oracle, you can start at the edge or perform a complete transformation.

Applications (SaaS): Oracle offers the most complete, innovative, and proven Cloud suite of SaaS applications that enable customers to transform their business with the latest intelligent technologies such as AI and machine learning.

Data (DaaS): Oracle Data Cloud provides data from a wide variety of Oracle and third-party sources, which can be used by sales and marketing to produce better business outcomes.

Platform (PaaS): Oracle offers the broadest range of PaaS services in the industry, which enable developers, IT professionals, and business leaders to develop, extend, and secure applications that leverage advanced analytics.

Infrastructure (IaaS): Oracle offers the highest performance, lowest cost IaaS in the industry, enabling customers to run their application workloads in the Oracle Cloud.

Oracle's complete suite is built on a single data model that connects end-to-end business processes and helps customers transform their business with intelligence.

Oracle empowers all sizes of companies, from startups to global enterprises.

Oracle Delivers Continuous Innovation to FUTURE PROOF Your Investment

Enhance your business IQ with adaptive intelligence. With decision science and machine learning embedded directly into business processes, business leaders can focus on managing their business outcomes rather than managing new technology. Examples include dynamic demand forecasts (SCM), personalized offers (CX), adaptive buy signals (ERP), and optimal candidates (HCM).

Utilize Internet of Things (IoT) cloud offerings to increase existing business application value with intelligent data and predictive analytics.

Leverage Oracle's mobile apps to manage the business and increase productivity while improving employee work-life balance through location flexibility.

Also, use Oracle's integrated cloud tools to extend or build new business processes.

Oracle Fusion Applications can best be described as:

- Built on an open standards-based platform
- Based on best practices business processes
- Deployed through a selection of options
- Built with security as a priority

Standards-Based Architecture

Oracle Fusion Applications is standards-based, making it highly adaptable. This standards-based technology enables you to respond effectively to change with flexible, modular, user-driven business software that is powered by best-in-class business capabilities built on open standards. Its technology framework includes the following products:

- Oracle WebCenter provides design-time and runtime tools for building enterprise portals, transactional websites, and social networking sites.
- Oracle Business Intelligence 11g provides a full range of business intelligence capabilities that enable you to analyze, present, report, and deliver organizational data.
- Oracle Universal Content Management enables you to leverage document management, Web content management, digital asset management; and records retention functionality to build and complement your business applications.
- Oracle SOA Suite provides a complete set of service infrastructure components for designing, deploying, and managing SOA composite applications. Oracle SOA Suite enables services to be created, managed, and orchestrated into SOA composite applications.
- Oracle WebLogic Server is a scalable, enterprise-ready application server based on Java Enterprise Edition (Java EE).

- Oracle JDeveloper is an integrated development environment with end-to-end support for modeling, developing, debugging, optimizing, and deploying Java applications and web services.
- Oracle Enterprise Manager offers business-driven applications management, integrated application to disk management, integrated systems management, and support experience.
- Oracle Identity Management enables organizations to manage the end-to-end lifecycle of user identities and to secure access to enterprise resources and assets.

Using a standards-based architecture reduces the cost for integration and enables you to reuse systems and technologies. Standards-based architecture also increases the flexibility of the applications. You can fit the applications to your business by configuring not only the user interface, but also the business objects, the business processes, the business logic, and business intelligence.

The ease of managing Oracle Fusion Applications offers a low total cost of ownership that results in a faster return on investment by using tools for rapid setup and flexible deployment models, as well as protecting upgrades.

Best Practices Business Processes

Oracle Fusion Applications incorporates best practices business processes, including those from Oracle product lines, such as Oracle E-Business Suite, PeopleSoft, Oracle On Demand, JD Edwards, and Siebel to optimize the user experience and productivity.

The Oracle Fusion Applications user interface facilitates the customer-driven, intuitive design of the applications that result in large productivity gains. The user interface design of Oracle Fusion Applications is:

- Role-based, which enables pervasive delivery in multiple modes, devices, and channels
- Configurable and extensible, through JDeveloper during design time or the composer during runtime, which enhances productivity for individual users and groups of users
- Composite and contextual, providing integrated information in the context of the process

- Social and collaborative, offering built-in user communities and workspace, Web 2.0 information distribution, and embedded social computing to improve collaborative work

Specific features of the user interface include:

- Role-based dashboards that you can configure to your business needs
- Unified worklists that provide lists of tasks from across the applications
- Guided Business Processes, which are organized sets of tasks that help you get your work done more efficiently
- Embedded analysis methods that provide the necessary information for completing a task
- Contextual help that provides conceptual and procedural reference information
- Oracle Fusion Applications Search, which provides a seamless search experience for easily locating and taking action on relevant data
- Tagging, which enables you to associate keywords with objects so they can be easily located
- Instant collaboration that provides the contact information for persons related to your tasks

Choice of Deployment Options

Oracle Fusion Applications is delivered as a suite but can be adopted modularly. It can be adopted as a single suite, as product offerings (the highest level collection of functionality that you can license and implement), or as solutions sets that work with other Oracle Applications Unlimited product lines.

Oracle Fusion Applications is offered with the following deployment options:

- On-premise, hosted by the enterprise
- Public cloud (available to the general public), hosted over the Internet by Oracle, software as a service (SaaS), or Oracle business partners offering business process outsourcing (BPO) solutions
- Private cloud (available internally behind a firewall), hosted as a SaaS or BPO offering

- Hybrid, an implementation of both on-premise and cloud

Security

Oracle Fusion Applications security offers:

- Role-based access
- Segregation of duties
- Consistent and transparent function and data security
- Robust privacy protections
- Native identity management and access provisioning
- Enforcement across tools (all the tools use the same policies) and across the information lifecycle
- Integration with Oracle Fusion Governance, Risk, and Compliance
- An extensive reference implementation
- Standard tools to extend the footprint

How the Modern Fusion Cloud application appears

- Interactive and Informative Dashboard

- All Financial data at One place

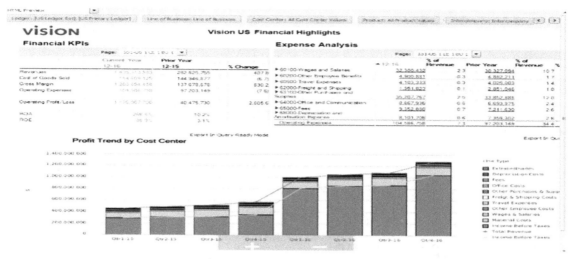

- Oracle connection with 3rd Party system made easy

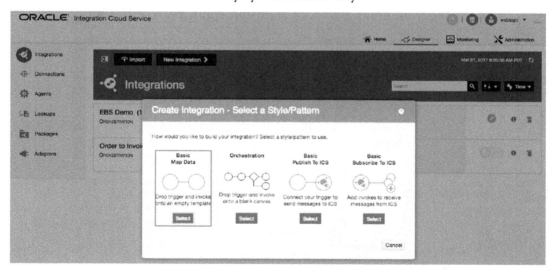

- Easy data Migration using advanced tools

Chart of Accounts, Calendar, and Ledger

*Required

*Name	Cosco India
Currency	USD
*Period Frequency	Monthly
*Adjusting Periods	None
*Fiscal Year Start Date	01/01/2016

Step 1: Validate

Step 2: Generate Chart of Accounts File

Step 3: Generate Ledger, LE, and BU File

Chart of Accounts

*Segment	Segment Label	*Short Prompt	*Display Width	
Company	Primary Balancing Segment	Company	4	Add Segment Sheets
Account	Natural Account Segment	Account	4	
Intercompany	Intercompany Segment	IC	4	

1.3 ON-PREMISE VS. CLOUD

Below are some of the technology advances of Fusion application from EBS

Technology	EBS	Fusion Cloud
Servers	Oracle Apps Server	Oracle Weblogic
GUI	Forms, JSP, OAF	Oracle ADF, ADF Java Server Faces
Workflow	PL/SQL	BPEL(Business Process Execution Language)
Reports	RDF/XML Publisher	BI Publisher
Analysis	Discoverer	OTBI(Oracle Transactional Business Intelligence)
Access	Responsibilities	Roles
Approvals	AME/Workflow	BPEL/BPM(Business Process Management)
Data Migration	Conversion	FBDI(File Based Data Import)
Setup/Configuration	Application	FSM(Functional Setup Manager)
Application Development	NA	Visual Builder- To Build Integrations, Extensions, Reports. Support Mobile & Voice UI

What's New	Benefits
Web based intuitive screen design	Reduce training efforts
Task driven workbench and Infolets	Improve productivity
Personalization capability	Improve agility
Mobile Apps for Transaction and Partners	Improve employee mobility and productivity/ Digitally connected to external parties
Transactional BI	Ad-hoc reports capability
Financial Report	Selectable point of views with drill-down capability
Excel Smart View	Slice and dice data for business analytics
Formatted Report	Formatted report with graphical presentation
Transactional dashboard	Provide key metrics
Accessible by managers &department users	Encourage direct accountability
Comprehensive FBDI templates	Improve and automate data entry tasks, reduce IT built costs
New Data APIs	Enable real-time data integration especially for client apps
New SOAP web services	Enable system integration with external applications
Configuration templates	Timesaver configuration tools
Comprehensive documentation	A centralized documentation repository improves accessibility to essential documents
Downloadable templates	Instant download for templates from web site or within applications
BPM Workflow (AMX)	Re-configurable Seeded workflow, Flexible rules to allow business simplification

The technical and functional changes are covered under subsequent chapters in details but the above tables will give you the summary of major differences.

FUSION ARCHITECTURE

2.1 INTRODUCTION TO FUSION ARCHITECTURE

As we have already seen, Fusion application brings together next-generation enterprise technologies, applications, and services, including Oracle Fusion Applications and Oracle Fusion Middleware, to fundamentally change the dynamics in the applications marketplace and revolutionize business. This chapter provides an introduction to the architecture, components, and concepts of Oracle Fusion Applications.

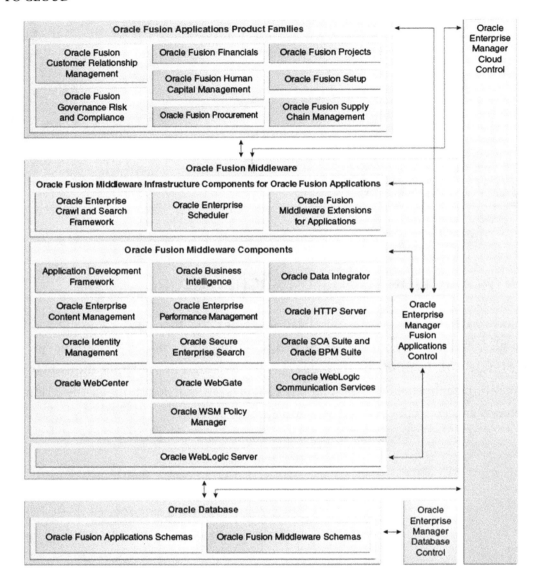

2.2 FUSION APPLICATION – PILLARS & OFFERINGS

Installation of Oracle Fusion Applications is logically broken up into groups of features known as product offerings, which represent the highest-level collection of functionality that you can license and implement. A provisioning configuration is a collection of one or more product offerings. During installation, you select a product offering or a combination of offerings as a way to install the product families.

Oracle Fusion Applications
7 Product Families, 100+ Modules

Oracle Fusion Financial Management			Oracle Fusion Human Capital Management			Oracle Fusion Supply Chain Management		
General Ledger	Accounts Payable	Asset Management	Global Human Resources	Workforce Lifecycle Management	Benefits	Product Master Data Management	Distributed Order Orchestration	Global Order Promising
Payments & Collections	Accounts Receivable	Cash & Expense Management	Compensation Management	Talent Review	Performance & Goal Mgmt	Inventory Management	Cost Management	Shipping & Receiving
Common Modules	KPIs, Dashboards, & Extensibility FW		Global Payroll	Network @ Work	KPIs, Dashboards, Extensibility	KPIs, Dashboards, & Extensibility FW		

Oracle Fusion Project Portfolio Management			Oracle Fusion Procurement			Oracle Fusion Customer Relationship Mgmt		
Project Costing	Project Billing	Project Performance Reporting	Purchasing	Self-service Procurement	Sourcing	Customer Master	Sales	Marketing
Project Control	Project Integration Gateway	Project Contracts	Procurement Contracts	Supplier Portal	Spend & Performance Analysis	Incentive Compensation	Mobile & Outlook Integration	Territory & Quota Mgmt
KPIs, Dashboards, & Extensibility FW			KPIs, Dashboards, & Extensibility FW			KPIs, Dashboards, & Extensibility FW		

Oracle Fusion Governance, Risk & Compliance	Financial Compliance	Issue & Risk Manager	Access Controls	Transaction Controls	Configuration Controls	KPIs, Dashboards, & Extensibility FW

☐ Oracle Fusion Customer Relationship Management

Manages customers, contacts, and resources, including data quality configuration.

☐ Oracle Fusion Financials

Manages financial flows, including assets, ledgers, cash cycle, invoices and payments, accounts receivable, collections, and setup of subledger accounting and tax configuration.

☐ Oracle Fusion Governance, Risk, and Compliance

Provides critical business controls to manage risk, multi-regulatory compliance and controls enforcement. The connector for Oracle Fusion Applications provides a prebuilt solution for managing the Separation of Duties (SoD) within and across product families. You can also utilize Oracle Fusion Governance, Risk, and Compliance to analyze suspect transactions and configuration settings based on user-defined conditions. This allows organizations to actively determine the risk that exists within their application that can materially impact the reliability of the information that exists for reporting and decision-making purposes.

☐ Oracle Fusion Human Capital Management

Provides employee management for an organization.

☐ Oracle Fusion Procurement

Manages the procurement process including requisitions, purchase orders, and supplier negotiations.

☐ Oracle Fusion Project

Manages projects, including how to plan, budget, forecast, collect costs, bill customers, and report performance.

☐ Oracle Fusion Supply Chain Management

Integrates and automates all key supply chain processes, from design, planning and procurement to manufacturing and fulfillment, providing a complete solution set to enable companies to power information-driven value chains.

☐ Oracle Fusion Setup

Supports the other product families. In addition to Oracle Fusion Functional Setup Manager for setting up functional data, this product family includes applications to assist application users:

The Oracle Fusion Home page provides a Welcome dashboard with a collection of portlets and task flows for answering common questions.

Oracle Fusion Applications Help delivers content users need to complete their tasks. You can optionally install a local version of Oracle Fusion Applications Help, enabling you to extend and customize the help.

2.3 ORACLE FUSION MIDDLEWARE INFRASTRUCTURE COMPONENTS

☐ Oracle Fusion Middleware Extensions for Applications (Applications Core)

Provides design time and runtime infrastructure to help standardize complex development patterns for Oracle Fusion Applications. It simplifies the development process of these patterns and provides a consistent user experience. Examples of these patterns include extensibility (Flexfields), hierarchical relationships (Trees), data security, and UI patterns. Applications Core creates simplified methods of implementing these complex requirements by providing robust metadata and comprehensive UI components and services. All of the Applications Core components have been intricately integrated with the rest of the Oracle Fusion Middleware infrastructure so they are available across every layer of the Oracle Fusion Applications platform.

Applications Core provides shared libraries referenced by all the Oracle Fusion Applications, a standalone application for application setup and configuration, an Oracle JDeveloper extension to seamlessly integrate our components with the rest of the Oracle Fusion Applications technology stack, PLSQL API's, C libraries, and common seed data.

☐ Oracle Enterprise Scheduler

Enables you to manage and schedule jobs for Oracle Fusion Applications.

☐ Oracle Enterprise Crawl and Search Framework (ECSF)

Oracle Enterprise Crawl and Search Framework (ECSF) enables Oracle Fusion Applications Search for performing full-text searches securely and simultaneously against multiple logical business objects. Any application that connects to multiple data sources or manages a significant amount of unstructured (non-database) information—or both—needs advanced search capabilities so that application users can easily locate and take action on data that is relevant to them.

2.4 ORACLE FUSION MIDDLEWARE COMPONENTS

☐ Oracle Application Development Framework (Oracle ADF)

Provides an end-to-end application framework that builds on Java Platform, Enterprise Edition (Java EE) standards and open-source technologies to simplify and accelerate implementing service-oriented applications.

☐ Oracle Business Intelligence

Oracle Business Intelligence provides a complete, integrated solution of analytics and reporting for Oracle Fusion Applications.

☐ Oracle Data Integrator

Extracts, transforms, and loads data for the product families.

☐ Oracle HTTP Server

It provides a web listener for applications and the framework for hosting static and dynamic pages and applications over the web. Based on the proven technology of the Apache HTTP Server, Oracle HTTP Server includes significant enhancements that facilitate load balancing, administration, and configuration.

☐ Oracle Identity Management

Provides a shared infrastructure for all applications, enabling developers to incorporate identity management into applications.

☐ Oracle SOA Suite

Provides a complete set of service infrastructure components for designing, deploying, and managing composite applications. Oracle SOA Suite enables services to be created, managed, and orchestrated into composite applications and business processes. Composites enable you to easily assemble multiple technology components into one SOA composite application.

An important component of Oracle SOA Suite is Oracle WSM Policy Manager. Oracle WSM Policy Manager provides the infrastructure for enforcing global security and auditing policies. By securing various endpoints and setting and propagating identity, it secures applications. Oracle WSM Policy Manager provides a standard mechanism for signing messages, performing encryption, performing authentication, and providing role-based access control. You also can change a policy without having to change the endpoints or clients for these endpoints, providing greater flexibility and security monitoring for your enterprise.

The Oracle Business Process Management (Oracle BPM) Suite provides an integrated environment for developing, administering, and using business applications centered on business processes. The Oracle BPM Suite is layered on the Oracle SOA Suite and shares many of the same product components.

☐ Oracle Secure Enterprise Search (Oracle SES)

Provides a search engine for Oracle Fusion Applications Search.

☐ Oracle WebCenter Content

Provides a comprehensive suite of digital content management tools. These tools can be used across the enterprise to cohesively track, manage, and dispose of content whether written, in digital images, or as email.

☐ Oracle WebCenter Portal

Enables you to create social applications, enterprise portals, collaborative communities, and composite applications, built on a standards-based, service-oriented architecture. Oracle WebCenter Portal combines dynamic user interface technologies with which to develop rich internet applications, the flexibility and power of an integrated, multichannel portal framework, and a set of horizontal Enterprise 2.0 capabilities delivered as services that provide content, collaboration, presence, and social networking capabilities. Based on these components, Oracle WebCenter Portal also provides an out-of-the-box, enterprise-ready customizable application, WebCenter Spaces, with a configurable work environment that enables individuals and groups to work and collaborate more effectively.

☐ Oracle WebGate

Acts as a communicator plug-in that accepts users' requests through Oracle HTTP Server and communicates with Oracle Access Manager.

☐ Oracle WebLogic Communication Services

Provides click-to-dial functionality for applications primarily through contextual actions. Contextual actions provide related information and actions to users within the immediate context of the object instances upon which they act.

☐ Oracle WebLogic Server

Supports the deployment of mission-critical applications in a robust, secure, highly available, and scalable environment. Oracle WebLogic Server is an ideal foundation for building applications based on service-oriented architecture (SOA).

2.5 ORACLE DATABASE AND OTHERS

The Oracle Database contains the schemas and tablespaces required for both the Oracle Fusion Applications and for your applications. Oracle Fusion Applications does not support other databases.

Oracle Fusion Applications encryption APIs mask data such as credit card numbers in application user interface fields. For encryption and masking beyond that, Transparent Data Encryption (TDE) and Oracle Database Vault (ODV) are certified but optional with Oracle Fusion Applications. TDE and ODV provide information lifecycle protections, such as the following:

- Data access restrictions on database administrators and other privileged users
- Sensitive data at rest in database files and file backups
- Sensitive data in transit
- Sensitive attributes in non-production databases

ODV establishes limitations on the power of privileged users to access sensitive data through the segregation of duties policies on DBA roles and by securely consolidating application data in the database. These limitations prevent DBAs and other privileged users from overriding the protections placed on sensitive data by the Virtual Private Database (VPD). Oracle Fusion Applications deploys with the ODV enabled when it is installed. TDE prevents access to PII in the file system or on backups or disk. TDE protects confidential data, such as credit card and social security numbers. TDE encrypts sensitive table data stored in data files at the tablespace level.

Oracle Enterprise Manager Fusion Applications Control

Oracle Enterprise Manager Fusion Applications Control (Fusion Applications Control) enables you to manage a single product family in an Oracle WebLogic Server domain for the Oracle Fusion Applications environment, including the products, applications, and Oracle Fusion Middleware components. As a part of management, you can monitor the runtime performance metrics for the various Oracle Fusion Applications and Oracle Fusion Middleware components.

Oracle Enterprise Manager Cloud Control

Oracle Enterprise Manager Cloud Control (Cloud Control) enables you to monitor and manage the complete IT infrastructure for Oracle Fusion Applications from a single console. You can monitor all the product families, Oracle Fusion Middleware components, and the Oracle Database. For example, you can monitor all the Oracle WebLogic Server domains for all the product families from one console.

Oracle Enterprise Manager Database Control

Oracle Enterprise Manager Database Control (Database Control) enables you to manage the Oracle Database. Using Database Control, you can perform administrative tasks such as creating schema objects (tables, views, indexes, and so on), managing user security, managing database memory and storage, backing up and recovering your database and importing and exporting data. You can also view performance and status information about your database.

Source: Oracle® Fusion Applications Administrator's Guide.

FUSION FINANCE

3.1 ORACLE FUSION FIXED ASSETS

Oracle Fusion Assets automates the asset management of the enterprise and simplifies the tasks involved in fixed asset accounting. It uses a unified source of assets data including data from Fusion Applications as well as external systems. It provides visibility into the complete assets data along with data security and function access.

Standard asset management tasks can be streamlined with the automated business flows for the below transactions.

- Asset Additions
- Asset transfer
- Disposals
- Reclassifications
- Financial adjustments
- Legacy data conversions

Introduction

Fusion Fixed Assets is integrated with the following applications:

- Fusion Payables
    - Assets can be created from Payables invoices by using the 'Create Mass Additions for Assets' process which will send valid invoice line distributions

and discounts from Payables to Mass Additions interface tables in Assets application.

- o The assets can be created in Assets application after reviewing the mass addition lines.

☐ Fusion Project Costing

- o Assets can be created from project lines in Project Costing using the flow given below:
- o Collect CIP costs for capital assets from Project Costing
- o Once the CIP asset is built, capitalize on the associated costs on the asset lines in Project Costing.
- o Run the 'Interface Assets' process. This will populate the mass additions interface table in Assets with the valid capital asset lines.
- o The assets can be created in Assets application after reviewing the mass addition lines.

☐ Fusion Subledger Accounting

- o Assets are integrated with Subledger Accounting for generating accounting entries, reporting and transactions drill down. The below steps should be followed for the SLA process.
- o Run 'Create Accounting for Assets' process for creating journal entries for the transaction events in Assets.
- o Transfer and post the journal entries to Oracle Fusion General Ledger.
- o Accounting reports can be used to review the asset information and reconcile to GL.

Overview of Asset Transactions

The Assets landing page contains the following infotiles:

Additions

Additions infotile represents the number of transactions that require action. They can have the statuses as Incomplete, Exceptions or Ready to Post. The number against each status indicates the number of transactions that require action. The Spreadsheet can also be used to update the transactions and then the assets can be directly posted from the Spreadsheet.

Posted assets can be included in the Asset Inquiry page along with other reports and accounting entries.

Adjustments

Adjustments infotile represents the Adjustments that are in progress. Old details, as well as the new details after the update, are available.

Transfers

Transfer infotile represents the details of the assets that are being transferred. Old details can be compared with the updated details using the Information icon.

Retirements

Retirements infotile represents the number of transactions that require action. They can have the statuses as Incomplete, Exceptions or Ready to Post. The Spreadsheet can also be used to update the transactions and then the assets can be directly posted from the Spreadsheet.

Depreciation

Once the actions such as Additions, Adjustments, Transfers and Retirements are complete, the 'Calculate Depreciation' process can be run. This can be used for

- Running Calculate Depreciation Process
- Running Calculate Depreciation Process and Closing the period.

Fixed Assets Import

Fixed Asset Mass Addition Import process can be used to upload multiple assets into Oracle Fusion Assets. Mass Additions spreadsheets can be downloaded using which the asset data can be prepared. The template has the instructions sheet as in other Fusion imports that will guide through the import process.

The import process can be used to Create Assets from the below sources:

- External sources, legacy systems
- Oracle Fusion Project Costing
- Oracle Fusion Payables

☐ Application Developer Framework (ADF) desktop integration spreadsheet.

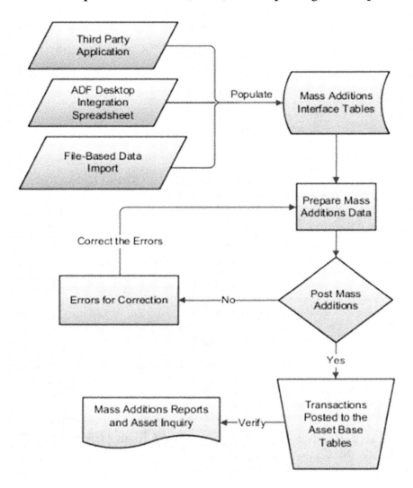

The below steps have to be followed for the import process.

☐ Navigate to File-Based Data Import for Oracle Financials Cloud guide.

☐ Click on File-Based Data Imports in the Table of Contents

☐ Click on Fixed Asset Mass Additions Import.

☐ Click on the link to the Excel template in the File Links section.

After the data is successfully loaded 'Post Mass Addition' process must be submitted to import the data into the application and create the assets.

☐ On the Assets page, click on the 'Ready to post link on Additions'.

☐ Click 'Post All'.

☐ Review the log file for any errors or warnings.

When the Post Mass Additions process is run, mass addition lines are processed according to the mass addition status they are assigned to.

Status Before Posting	Status After Posting
Post	Posted
Cost Adjustment	Posted
Merged	Posted
Split	Split
New	New
On Hold	On Hold
Delete	Delete

Assets Reporting

Oracle Fusion Assets provides predefined reports that are used in the close process to verify asset transactions. They are run from the Scheduled Processes work area. Some of the reports are listed below.

Report Name	Description
Asset Additions Report	Displays all the assets added or capitalized during the specific period
Asset Retirements Report	Displays all the asset retirements performed during the specific period

Asset Transaction History Report	Displays all transactions performed on the selected assets
Asset Transfer Report	Displays all asset transfers performed during the specific period
Cost Adjustment Report	Displays asset cost adjustments made during the specific period
Create Mass Additions Report	Displays all invoice and discount lines processed by the last run of the Create Mass Additions Process.
Cost Detail Report	Displays asset level asset cost account balances for the specified periods
Reserve Summary Report	Displays reserve account summary balances for the specified periods
Reserve Detail Report	Displays asset level reserve account balances for the specified periods

3.2 ORACLE FUSION RECEIVABLES

Introduction to Fusion Receivables

Oracle Fusion Receivables provides an integrated functionality for performing the accounts-receivables operations. Fusion Receivables is managed using the work areas of Billing, Receivables Balances and Revenue Management. The work areas provide access to GL accounting activities like Create Accounting, Creating and Editing Journal entries, etc.

Billing Work Area

The billing work area is used for performing customer billing-related activities that include monitoring and reviewing transactions, approving pending adjustments, importing transactions from other systems using AutoInvoice like invoices or credit memos, etc.

Errors in the AutoInvoice process can be reviewed and corrected for resubmission. Customer data can also be created and managed in this work area.

Receivables Balances Work Area

Receivables Balances work area is used for performing activities related to customer payments and also to manage receivables balances. Open receipts, receipt batches, unapplied and on-account receipts, credit memos, receipt remittance batches and funds transfer errors. Activities related to managing receipts including receipt remittances, receipt remittance batches can be performed. Also, tasks related to managing accounts receivables balances like reconciling receivables and managing receivable accounting period statuses can be performed.

Revenue Management Work Area

Revenue Management work area is used for performing activities related to revenue recognition and revenue adjustments. Recognize Revenue program is run to generate revenue distribution records for invoices and credit memos. Revenue adjustments can be performed on transactions including reviewing, adding and expiring revenue contingencies and transferring sales credits. Revenue policies and rules to assign revenue contingencies to transactions automatically can also be handled.

Billing and Receivables Balances Work area – both have access to manage customer data/ account information at summary and detail level. For each customer, the corresponding transactions and receipts, dispute and adjust transactions and drill-down to the current/ historical activities can be viewed.

Key Features of Fusion Receivables

- ☐ Auto Lockbox SmartReceipts – Auto Lockbox feature has been enhanced to apply receipts automatically using SmartReceipts in Fusion Receivables.
- ☐ Receipts are matched with the invoices correctly based on system recommendations that include exception handling.
- ☐ This functionality has been extended to receipts that are either manually created or loaded into Fusion as Customer Receipts.

- ☐ Payment information is used for applying receipts to make the best possible matches.
- ☐ Invoices are prioritized and displayed to the users based on the matching rules defined.
- ☐ AutoMatch Rule Set uses options such as Minimum Weighted Threshold, Days of Closed Invoices Threshold, Combined Weighted Threshold and Customer Recommendation Threshold.
- ☐ Excel-based receipt entry which is easy to process and exceptions are automatically identified.
- ☐ Leverage Excel functionality and share spreadsheets with reviewers and approvers.

Smart Receipts

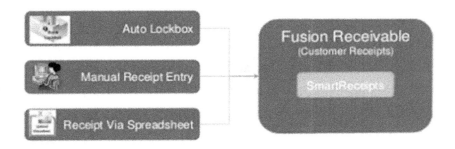

AutoMatch Rule Set

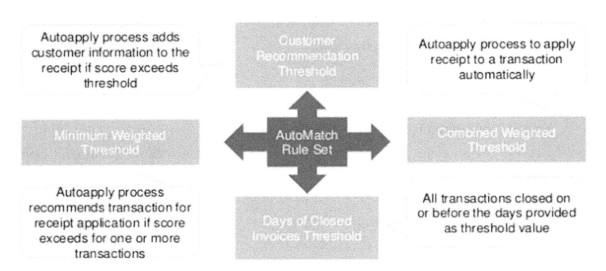

Fusion Receivables Reports

Reporting in Fusion Receivables cover the below areas:

- ☐ Bill Presentment Templates
- ☐ Accounting Reports
- ☐ Billing Reports
- ☐ Receivables Balances Reports
- ☐ Bills Receivables Reports
- ☐ Netting Settlement Reports
- ☐ Reconciliation Program Reports

Receivables reports are run from Scheduled Processes work area and also from the Reports and Analytics page.

- ☐ Click on the Schedule New Process button.
- ☐ Search for the Process Name as shown in the dialog box below.
- ☐ Enter values for the parameters based on the report
- ☐ Enter the process options and schedule and then click on Submit.

Process Details   ✕

ⓘ This process will be queued up for submission at position 1

[Process Options]   [Advanced]   [Submit]   [Cancel]

Name	Billing History Report
Description	Lists a summarized history of transactions and ...
Schedule	As soon as possible

☐ Print output

☐ Notify me when this process ends

Submission Notes

Basic Options

Parameters

* Business Unit	▼
From Customer Name	▼
To Customer Name	▼
From Customer Account Number	▼
To Customer Account Number	▼
From Transaction Number	
To Transaction Number	
From Collector Name	▼
To Collector Name	▼
From Payment Terms	▼
To Payment Terms	▼

3.3 ORACLE FUSION PAYABLES

Introduction to Fusion Payables

Oracle Fusion Payables provides the integrated functionality for providing accounts-payables activities including payments for products and services, details of accounts, vendors, resolving issues and improving the flow of goods and payments. It covers the processes of Invoicing, Payments, Fusion Expenses, iSupplier, Accounting in Fusion Payables, etc.

Procure-to-Pay Process

The Procure-to-Pay process begins with the identification of the requirement and authorizing the purchase request. Vendor selection and negotiation processes follow this after which the purchase order is placed with the vendor. The goods are then received from the supplier and inspected for the matching PO quantity. An invoice will be recorded now to match the purchase order or the receipt. This invoice has to be approved for the payment to be scheduled. The supplier will then be paid.

The business processes involved in Fusion Payables are listed below:

Payables setup is available under the Financial and Procurement offerings. Function security is implemented using Job roles and data security is implemented using the data roles. Pre-defined job roles used for Payables job functions are Accounts Payable Specialist, Accounts Payable Supervisor and Accounts Payable Manager. Payables job roles are configured to maintain segregation of duties for managing suppliers, invoices and payments. Custom data roles can be created using the seeded data role template for the business units. Pre-defined job roles and duty roles can be customized using Oracle Identity Manager (OIM) and Access Provisioning Manager (APM).

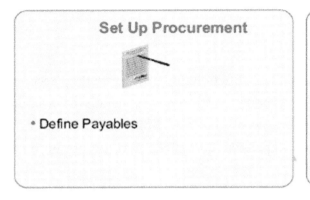

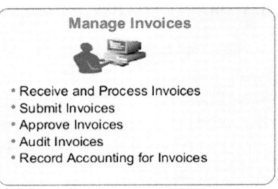

Set Up Procurement

• Define Payables

Manage Invoices

• Receive and Process Invoices
• Submit Invoices
• Approve Invoices
• Audit Invoices
• Record Accounting for Invoices

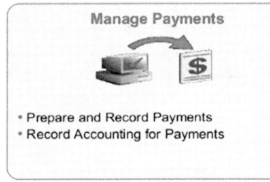

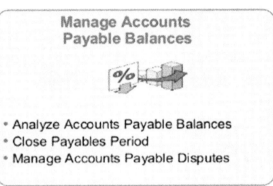

Manage Payments

• Prepare and Record Payments
• Record Accounting for Payments

Manage Accounts Payable Balances

• Analyze Accounts Payable Balances
• Close Payables Period
• Manage Accounts Payable Disputes

Key Features of Fusion Payables

Integrated Imaging Solution

The imaging solution in Fusion Payables is fully integrated with the application and supports the entire lifecycle of invoice processing from scanning, recognition, image routing to invoice entry and approval. It is maintained by the common provisioning framework that requires minimal configurations and setups.

The solution helps in digitizing paper invoices to industry-standard image formats. It supports enterprise-class scanners and high-volume document scanning interfaces. It has flexible implementation options for scanning invoices at multiple field offices.

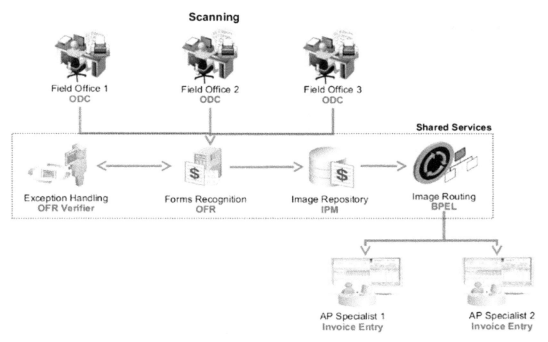

☐ Requests are sent to suppliers to send invoices to one central location for scanning (Decentralize ODC) at each invoice receipt location.

☐ Intelligent data extraction without using supplier-specific templates.

☐ Self-learning intelligence to improve scan accuracy over time.

☐ User-configurable validation of the images with Payables and Procurement data.

☐ A common image repository is available where images are stored and then routed to the payables team.

☐ The embedded image viewer is available in Fusion Payables to allow users to review images.

☐ Fusion Payables provides default image-based routing rule based on the invoice amounts. Routing rules can also be assigned to a group instead of a single user.

☐ Multiple Invoice entry methods are available such as Supplier Portal Invoice Entry, Evaluated Receipt Settlement, Spreadsheet Invoice Entry and Open Interface.

Manual Invoice Entry

✓ Invoice Scanning and Imaging

✓ Robust Workbench with Sophisticated Matching

✓ Spreadsheet Invoice Entry

✓ Open Interface

Self-Service Invoice Entry

✓ Supplier Portal

Payables Invoicing

- Foreign Currency Conversion
- PO/Receipt Matching
- Prepayment Application
- Automatic Tax Calculation (Sales, Use, VAT, and Withholding Taxes)
- Invoice Validation
- Invoice Approval
- Online or Batch Accounting
- Multiple Accounting Representations

Automated Invoicing

✓ ERS (Self-Billing) Invoices

✓ Return to Supplier (RTS)

✓ Expense Reports

✓ Customer Refunds

✓ Intercompany Invoices

Electronic Invoices

✓ Web Service

✓ B2B Invoice

Approval levels 2-way, 3-way and 4-way matching are available to ensure payment is made against the goods and services offered. Unmatched approval level is also available for legal services or utility bills and payment requests for employee expense reports.

Fusion Tax

Oracle Fusion Tax is a centralized tax engine that can be quickly set up with the pre-seeded content. Tax changes can be simulated using the Tax Simulator. Tax calculations are made automatically and accurately but it also allows certain users to override the calculations.

Sales and Use Tax

Recoverable & Non-Recoverable Tax

Deferred Tax

Tax on Freight

Duty Tax

Tax on Intercompany Movements

Inclusive or Exclusive Tax

Offset Taxes

Fusion Payables Reports

Reporting in Fusion Payables cover the below areas:

- ☐ Invoices
- ☐ Payments
- ☐ Payables to Ledger Reconciliation
- ☐ Period Close
- ☐ Prepayments
- ☐ Income Tax and Withholding
- ☐ Netting

They are run from the Scheduled Processes work area. Some of the reports are listed below.

Report Name	Description
Import Payables Invoices Report	Report from the import process of invoice data
Payables Invoice Aging Report	Displays unpaid invoices during the specific aging period
Supplier Balance Aging Report	Displays unpaid supplier invoices during the specified aging period
Payables Invoice Register	Displays detail information about invoices

Payables Cash Requirement Report	Immediate cash needs for invoice payments
Payables Payment Register	Displays detail information about payments
Payables to Ledger Reconciliation Report	Displays the journals posted to General Ledger for open payables balances to help in the reconciliation of accounting and transactional data in Payables and Subledger Accounting
Payables Period Close Exceptions Report	Displays exceptions in Payables period close process
Payables Trial Balance Report	Displays all unpaid and partially paid invoices that Payables transferred to the General Ledger

3.4 ORACLE FUSION GENERAL LEDGER

Introduction

Oracle Fusion General Ledger combines the traditional general ledger functionality with dimension based reporting functionality embedded from Oracle Essbase Technology. The balance cube is automatically created when the ledgers are set up in Fusion application and the accounting configuration is complete. Any changes done to the configurations are automatically updated in the dimensions using simple maintenance routines. Then when the transactions are posted, the multi-dimensional cube gets updated automatically. Requirements for using batch programs to update the cubes regularly are not valid anymore.

At every possible level, balances are aggregated in the dimensions of the chart of accounts and the accounting periods across hierarchies which results in the reporting and inquiry. When the entry is posted, Reports and Analytics are refreshed immediately without any programs to be run. This is because the cubes are already updated and aggregated at all levels. The multi-dimensional analysis is also instantaneous that reports can be viewed instantly using different dimensions on the same data along with drill-down options.

Oracle Fusion Accounting Hub

Oracle Fusion Accounting Hub leverages the Oracle Fusion General Ledger. Accounting Hub provides a prebuilt integration with Oracle EBS with the help of Open API. Accounting Hub takes care of creating the appropriate accounting to meet statuary, corporate, regulatory and management reporting in a controlled and consistent manner. The Accounting Hub has exceptional reporting and analytics platform that can be leveraged with minimal implementation effort.

Benefits of using Fusion Accounting Hub

- Risk reduction – Option for continuing with EBS for other processes like procure-to-pay or credit-to-collections without disruption. No changes required in accounting treatment in EBS.
- Coexistence of Fusion Accounting Hub with Fusion General Ledger helps in reducing costs while using next-generation Fusion Applications.

Features of Fusion Accounting Hub

- It uses Fusion General Ledger to process journal transactions that are posted to update General Ledger Balances.
- Fusion Subledger Accounting Rules Engine is used to account for transactions from the Sub ledgers like Payables, Receivables, Assets, and Inventory, etc. after applying the desired treatment.
- Advanced Intercompany Accounting capabilities for managing Intercompany transactions.
- Reporting and Analytics tool to provide useful reports for fulfilling business requirements.
- Drill-down capabilities to view summarized balances and also to trace transactions to the originating transaction details.
- Allocation engine to support complex formulas in journal entries.

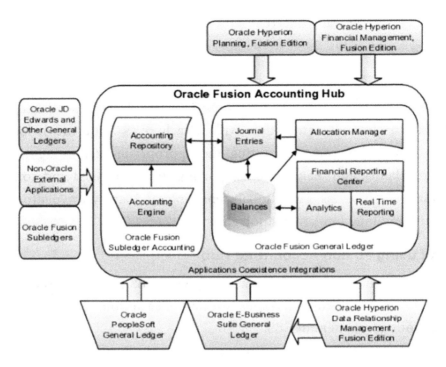

Subledger Accounting captures the events, accounts for them under different accounting conventions, posts them in detail or summary to Oracle Fusion General Ledger, and stores them in financially oriented and standardized accounting subledgers.

Oracle Fusion General Ledger tracks the accounting at a distilled level that is specified by you and preaggregates the balances in the balances cube. The Financial Reporting Center provides financial reporting and inquiry with the Account Monitor and Account Inspector. Smart View provides spreadsheet analytics and Oracle Transaction Business Intelligence, Oracle Business Intelligence Analytics, and Oracle Business Intelligence Publisher provide key performance indicators (KPI), dashboards, and flexible reporting.

Fusion General Ledger Features

The General Ledger dashboard presents information that users need to know and also the actions that have to be taken to move through the application. Embedded data tabulations provide the information required for decision making.

The General Ledger Account Hierarchies leverage the common date effective tree model in Fusion Applications. A segment in the chart of accounts can have multiple hierarchies and each hierarchy can have multiple versions.

Allows to have 3 balancing segments – Balancing segment is a segment in the chart of accounts that generates receivable and payable balancing entries between the different values in the segment when the entry crosses those values. The effect is to allow equity to be tracked accurately in each segment.

Reporting in Fusion General Ledger

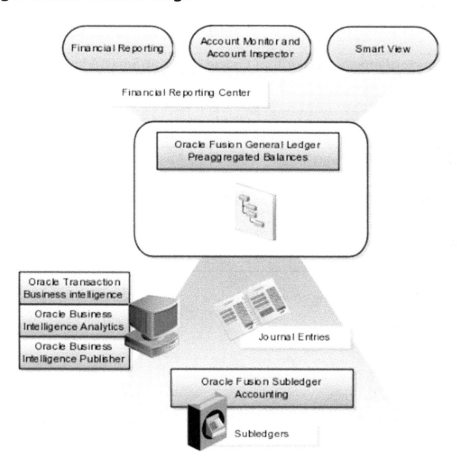

Oracle Fusion General Ledger provides excellent reporting capabilities. The posting process in General Ledger updates the balances and these balances are stored in the cubes for multi-dimensional analysis. The Financial Reporting Center provides an inquiry and reporting through the Financials Reports Functionality and the Account Monitor. The product work areas provide information on the tasks to be performed. Account Monitor is available in the General Ledger dashboard and Financial Reporting Center.

The solution provided by Fusion Financials for some of the major financial needs are listed below

Report Requirement	Solution
Financial Statements with live drill-down	Financial Reporting in the Financial Reporting Center
Spreadsheet financial reports with drill down	Oracle Hyperion Smart View for Office
Ad Hoc queries for transactions	OTBI
KPIs, Metrics from the data warehouse	Oracle BI Analytics
High volume operational reporting with multi-dimensional analysis, pivoting and drill down	Oracle BI Publisher

Fusion General Ledger reporting covers the below areas:

- Account Analysis
- Journals
- Trial Balance Reports
- Reconciliation Reports
- Chart of Accounts

Some of the General Ledger reports include the following:

Report Name	Description
Account Analysis	Report to print balances from the account segment and a secondary segment for each journal entry.
General Ledger Account Details Report	Displays journal information to trace each transaction to the original source
Journals Report	Displays journal activity for a specified period
Journals Batch Summary Report	Displays posted journal batches for a particular period
Journals Details Report	Displays information about manual entered journals prior to posting
Trial Balance Report	Displays summarized actual account balances and activity by ledger
Cash to General Ledger Reconciliation Report	Extracts cash management and general ledger accounting and transactional data for reconciling cash management to General Ledger
Payables to Ledger Reconciliation Report	Summarized and detailed reconciling data for review. Displays payables and accounting beginning and ending balances.
Receivables to Ledger Reconciliation Report	Reconciliation of receivables data to General Ledger. Displays receivables and accounting beginning and ending balances.

FUSION SCM

4.1 INVENTORY MANAGEMENT CLOUD

Introduction to Inventory Cloud

Oracle Inventory Management for Cloud comprises the complete material management solution to enable companies to successfully handle the movement of goods, both inbound and outbound.

What are the benefits?

- ☐ Reduces inventory levels
- ☐ Single source of truth for Inventory
- ☐ Efficiently manage receipts and received lines
- ☐ Streamline the flow of materials

Fusion Inventory Objectives

- ☐ Minimize Inventory levels
- ☐ Complete Inventory Visibility
- ☐ Inventory Accuracy

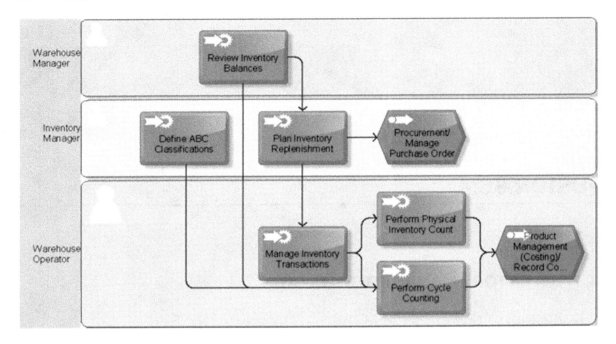

Inventory Organizations form the basics of Oracle Inventory and represent the distinct entity in the enterprise where items are stored and transactions happen. They have to be defined to start using Oracle Inventory.

Inventory Organization can be

- ☐ Master org – Logical entity
- ☐ Warehouse – Physical entity

Inventory Organization attributes

- ☐ Have own ledger, location, items, costing method, etc.
- ☐ Share characteristics with other organizations (org)

Inventory Organization Structure

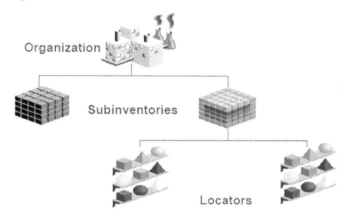

Subinventory

One or more Subinventories → Inventory Org

Grouping of the material inventory like raw material, finished goods, defective goods, etc.

At least one subinventory has to be defined mandatorily for every Inventory Org. to transact items.

Item quantities can be tracked or restricted based on the subinventory.

Mandatory Information:

- ☐ Unique name
- ☐ Status
- ☐ Parameters
- ☐ Lead Times
- ☐ Sourcing Information

Locator

One or more Locators → Subinventories

Locators are physical areas where the inventory items are stored.

Items can be tracked or restricted based on the locators.

Useful Features in Fusion Inventory

On-Hand Quantity

- ☐ Review Item Supply and Demand – summary on on-hand quantity, incoming and outgoing demand
- ☐ Quantities to include – All, Nettable Only, ATP Only
- ☐ Supply types – On-hand quantity, Purchase Order quantity, Purchase Orders, Purchase Requisitions, etc.
- ☐ Demand Types – Sales orders, Transfer orders, Shipment lines, outside processing orders, etc.

Key Terms:

Nettable quantities are for fulfilling demand and included in on-hand quantity.

Nonnettable quantities are not for fulfilling demand and not included in on-hand quantity.

Manage Material Transactions

- ☐ Subinventory Transactions – Transfer material within the organization between subinventories.
- ☐ Miscellaneous Transactions – Misc. Issue or Misc. Receipt where documentation is not available/ required. Used for making ad-hoc adjustments to on-hand quantities.
- ☐ E-Signature Approval – E-Signatures can be used for approving Misc. transactions
- ☐ Inter-organization Transfers – transfer material between inventory organizations
  - o Direct – move items between inventory organizations
  - o In-Transit – move items from source organization to in-transit inventory.
- ☐ Movement Request – Requests for moving material within an inventory organization.
  - o Requisition Movement
  - o Replenishment Movement
  - o Shop Floor Movement
- ☐ Warehouse Operations Dashboard
- ☐ Warehouse KPIs
- ☐ Picking/ Shipping/ Receiving Work-areas

- Integrated Procurement, Cost Management, Distributed Order Orchestration and Product Management
- Real-time information on Inventory Balances, Transactional Reporting and Dashboards

High-level Overview

- Consolidate inventory tracking into a global solution
- Efficiently manage inventory information for different types of materials
- Multi-dimensional inventory analysis
- Proactively monitor inventory levels
- Effectively manage the flow of goods – inbound & outbound

Dashboard for Inventory Management

- Monitor the KPIs for Warehouse operations
- Compare KPIs with one another/ compare data from different periods
- Several drill-down reports to have a complete 360-degree view of inventory information.
- Tasks to perform/ action items easily identified.

WEBADI vs. ADFdi

ADFdi user interface desktop integration is a feature similar to WebADI available in EBS. This feature enables us to load data from EXCEL Spreadsheet directly into Oracle Fusion. In Inventory Reservations, Data can be loaded into Fusion Applications through ADFdi.

4.2 PROCUREMENT CLOUD

Introduction to Fusion Applications

Oracle Fusion Applications are an integrated suite of business applications that automates all the end-to-end business processes and addresses the need for a global enterprise. It is designed in such a way that enterprises can be modeled to meet legal and management objectives. All the setup related processes can be streamlined by sharing common setup data across the applications.

Oracle Fusion Procurement

Oracle Fusion Procurement is a set of applications designed to provide complete procurement solutions or extensions to the existing procurement applications. Using the latest technology for Procurement results in improved performance, lower IT costs and better reporting.

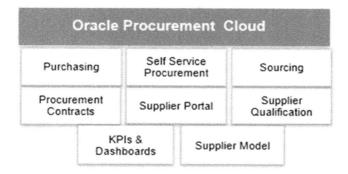

It is important for corporates to streamline and strategize the procurement business operations to reflect in the revenue of the enterprise. Oracle Fusion Procurement as part of the Oracle Supply Chain Management provides a lot of advantages to the businesses.

It provides insights into different procurement activities for various users in the organizational hierarchy.

Workflow defined in Fusion Procurement helps in providing the right set of information to the right users during the entire life cycle of the procurement process.

In addition to covering the end to end procurement business operations, Fusion Procurement also provides user-friendly dashboards that provide role-based information to prioritize procurement actions. The dashboards provide relevant business intelligence reports on procurement information with embedded analytics. These reports help in identifying opportunities that might result in additional business, align strategies to the business goals and also monitor areas that require attention.

Fusion Procurement Applications provide contract standards that are simple yet follow global standards and have the flexibility to be used by any business. It provides options to enforce business policies using contract templates and towards contract creation. The contract repository is maintained with Search options and automated renewal options. Complete audit history is also maintained with amendments and addendums.

Integrated Sourcing and Contract management capabilities help in negotiation contracts and agreements, prioritizing actions for procurement and areas of cost savings. It seamlessly handles the collaboration of the internal and external parties for all the compliance necessary to be in place. It improves requirement gathering, document sharing and negotiation effectiveness.

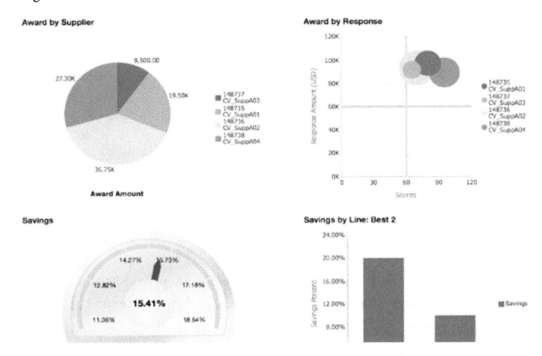

Important Features of Procurement Cloud

User Interface features in Fusion procurement for end uses are highly efficient and easy to use. It enhances the shopping experience of the users and user satisfaction. There are several features such as Search options, recent transaction history, tagging, embedded learning, etc. that make the application very user-friendly. The application is designed in such a way that the routine tasks of procurement operations are dramatically reduced and the attention of users is required for improvement areas that are highlighted.

A user-friendly interface is also provided to the suppliers by the expansion of self-service in Oracle procurement.

The requisition process is automated with Invoice matching and payment options.

Suppliers can be qualified and assessed for compliance and negotiation of awards. Timely updates to supplier information are done to ensure information accuracy.

Enhanced supplier collaboration is provided by allowing the sharing of documents and all transactions done electronically.

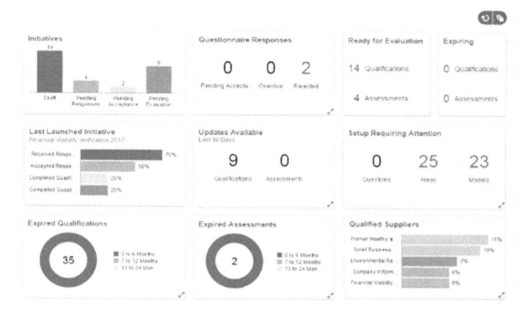

Oracle Fusion Procurement Setup Flow

The following diagram illustrates the various configurations in Fusion Applications for implementing Procurement Cloud.

The following Setup Tasks are involved in the Procurement implementation.

- ☐ Common Applications Configuration for Procurement
- ☐ Common Procurement Configuration
- ☐ Purchasing Configuration
- ☐ Self Service Procurement Configuration
- ☐ Supplier Portal Configuration
- ☐ Sourcing Configuration
- ☐ Procurement Contracts Configuration
- ☐ Supplier Qualification Configuration

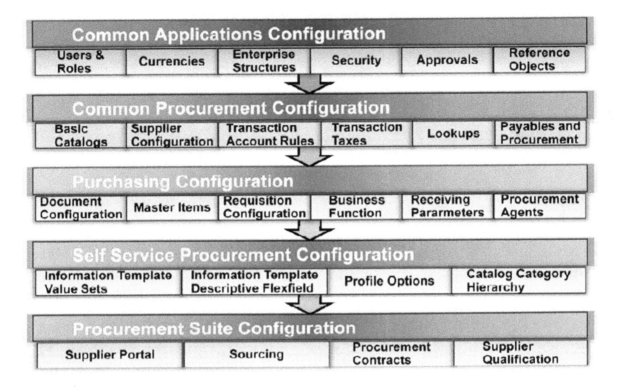

Conclusion

The above-mentioned cloud solutions under Oracle Fusion procurement that provide business process flows supporting the Procure to pay process can be deployed as a single complete solution or as an enhanced feature of an existing application to add on to the Procurement capabilities. There are various advantages to migrating to the Oracle procurement cloud. One of the main reasons would be to have a single source of truth for procurement data especially Contracts that require to be adhered to by compliances and policies. There are also significant cost savings in migrating to Oracle Procurement Cloud. The internal and external relationships are well maintained electronically that drives the negotiation process and awards to be effective. This real-time collaboration between the stakeholders results in avoiding delays in Procurement and also in avoiding risks. All processes in Procurement are managed through automated workflows that also provide flexibility in designing/ customizing the business processes.

4.3 ORDER MANAGEMENT CLOUD

Introduction

Oracle Order Management Cloud is designed to improve order capture and fulfillment execution across the quote to cash process by providing a central order hub for multi-channel environments. The application provides the ability to capture, price and configure orders through direct order entry. Orders can also be received from external sources, modified and then processed for fulfillment. It also provides pre-built integrations with other Oracle Cloud services, centrally managed orchestration policies, global availability, and fulfillment monitoring.

Source: Oracle Order Management Cloud Data Sheet

Key Features of Order Management Cloud

- Omni channel Order to Cash Management
  - Centralize and manage multiple order capture channels, do order promising, orchestrate fulfillment policies, monitor order status, manage exceptions, enter, price, and configure sales orders directly in Order Management.
  - Receive source orders from external sources, modify them in Order Management, and then process them for fulfillment.
  - Predefined integrations with other Oracle cloud services to centrally manage orchestration policies, get global availability, monitor statuses, and manage exceptions.
- Single Face to Customer – Unified customer-facing processes and consolidated view of the customers
- End-to-End Capability- OM Cloud can be Automated, monitored, and managed the process from order capture to settlement to post-sales care.
- Optimized Order Scheduling - Orders can be Fulfilled from the most profitable source and utilize global inventory
- Allocate Supply – Serve the markets by allocating supply based on attributes of customer, order, or item.

- Prioritize Backlog - Consolidated view can be Managed for backlog and reprioritize the orders
- Pre-Seeded Processes – Process like drop-ships, back-to-back, capable-to-promise, configure-to-order, and more can be enabled
- Touchless Orchestration - Order fulfillment processes for products as well as services on the same order can be Defined and executed
- End-to-End Visibility – Visibility on Order Updates, inventory, shipments, planned supply, and invoices, and improve the quality of decisions
- Exception Resolution
  - Monitor - Keep tabs on fulfillment tasks and resolve issues before they affect customer
  - What-if Analysis - View and evaluate various options before picking the best one
  - Order Changes - Define and enforce rules for changing orders

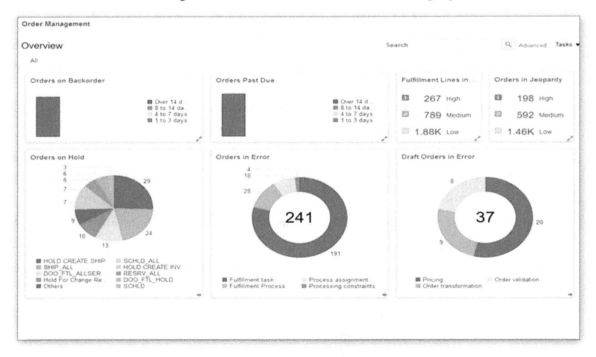

ORACLE OM Cloud – Overview Dashboard

Cloud Order Management – An Improvement over EBS OM

The typical Order to cash process flow will be like below in sequence

- ☐ Create Sales Order
- ☐ Submit Sales Order
- ☐ Create Pick Wave
- ☐ Confirm Pick Slip
- ☐ Ship Confirm
- ☐ Run Workflow Background Process
- ☐ Run Auto Invoice Master program
- ☐ Invoice created in Receivables

But in Order management cloud application three important processes are included to make the O2C more robust

- ☐ Sales Order Fulfillment
- ☐ Global Order Promising
- ☐ Order Orchestration process.

Let's see the overall flow and how it works in Oracle cloud application

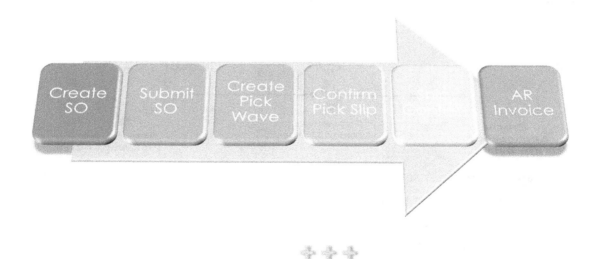

✤ ✤ ✤

OM Cloud – Process Flow

The following diagram illustrates how Order Management can transform a source order to a sales order, reply with a confirmation, and then orchestrate fulfillment tasks for this sales order, such as schedule, reserve, ship, and bill. It also updates the fulfillment line status while it does this work, and then sends it periodically to the order capture system.

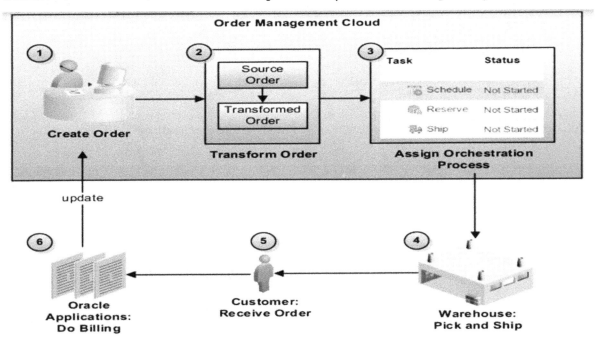

☐ **Capture orders**. A source system that resides outside of Order Management Cloud sends a source order to Order Management.

☐ **Transform orders**. The transformation layer uses transformation rules to transform the source order into a sales order that Order Management can process, and then assigns an orchestration process to this sales order. Transformation separates the source order into a data hierarchy that Order Management can recognize. You can set up transformation rules that meet your specific transformation requirements. **Orchestrate orders**. The orchestration layer uses one or more orchestration processes to run the fulfillment step, and then send the sales order to the task layer.

☐ **Perform tasks**. The task layer sends the request to the external interface layer. The task layer includes services that can send a request to perform a fulfillment task to a fulfillment system. Order Management provides services that can perform some of the more typical fulfillment system work, such as shipping or invoicing.

☐ **Integrate**. The external interface layer does the following work.
  o Cross-references the data that the request contains.
  o Uses routing rules to identify the fulfillment system to use to fulfill each fulfillment line.

☐ **Fulfill**. The fulfillment system processes the request.
  o The fulfillment system accepts the request, and then sends a reply.
  o The external interface layer converts the reply from the fulfillment system.
  o The task layer processes the reply from the fulfillment system.
  o The orchestration layer runs the next fulfillment step.

Source: Order Management Implementation Guide

Orchestration Process

Order Orchestration uses an orchestration process that identifies and assigns the set of steps that it will use to fulfill the order. Orchestration process can be set up to meet the requirements of our organization. Specify the rules that determine how Order Management Cloud creates the orchestration process at run time and then assigns objects to fulfillment lines that Order Management creates as part of order processing

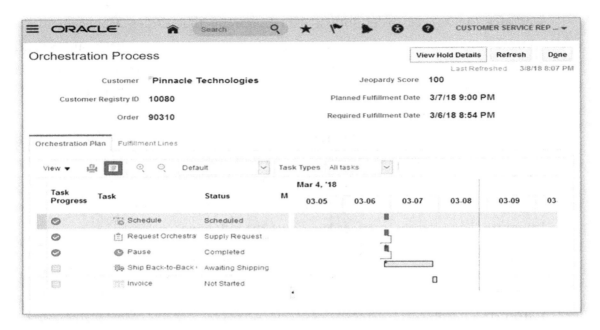

An orchestration process provides a way for you to define a business process. It can include steps that call the task layer service, get planning details, modify change management settings, set status conditions, and so on

Order Orchestration also does the following work.

- References data in the Oracle Product Model to determine the item data to use for the order.
- References Oracle Business Rules that specify how to orchestrate each order. You can define a variety of rules.
- References data that resides in the Order Management and Planning Data Repository to cross-reference and validate data. To collect this data, you define data collection parameters, enable data for collections, and so on
- Sequences the fulfillment steps that process the order.
- Calls the task layer services. You can determine how an orchestration process calls a task layer service.

Global Order Promising

Oracle Order Management Cloud's global order promising features help us to satisfy the most demanding customers by scheduling delivery based on actual supply across all potential sources including production capacity and purchases from suppliers

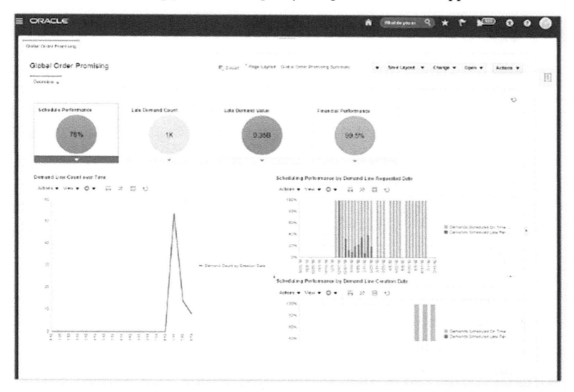

An orchestration process interacts with Oracle Global Order Promising Cloud to determine availability and to promise the order. Global Order Promising Cloud does the following work.

- ☐ Uses supply and demand data from the Order Management and Planning Data Repository to determine availability in the supply chain, such as inventory levels in warehouses.
- ☐ Schedules the best fulfillment options for each fulfillment line. A user can also manually use the Order Management work area to determine and choose these options.

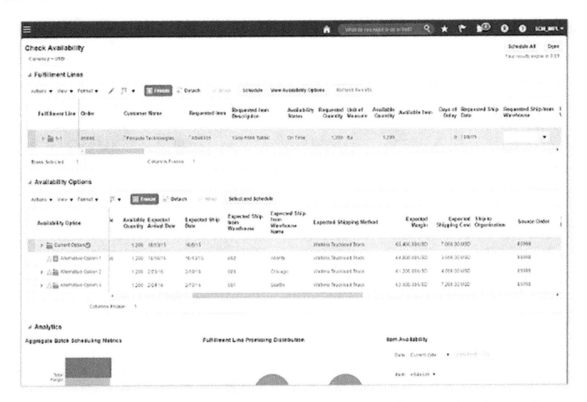

☐ Communicates with Oracle Shipping to ship the order. For details, see Shipping: How it Works.

☐ Updates the fulfillment status.

☐ Sends order information to order billing.

☐ If the order must reserve the item, then Order Management interacts with Oracle Inventory Management.

Fulfillment Lines

Om Cloud runs the orchestration process steps and manages fulfillment tasks.

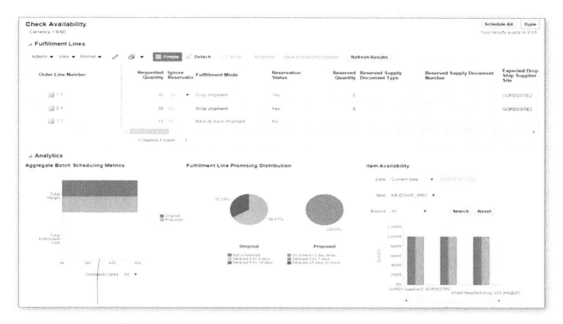

It communicates with Global Order Promising so that it can cross-reference items before it sends the message to downstream fulfillment systems through the External Interface Layer. For instance, it sends a shipment request to the shipping system; an orchestration process can call the Shipment Task Layer service to create a shipment request.

Oracle fulfillment systems do the following work.

- ☐ Oracle Materials Management Cloud manages logistics and inventory for the order, including schedule, reserve, receive, and ship each item.
- ☐ Accounts Receivables processes the billing information, including one-time charges and recurring charges, and then sends this information to Oracle Financials Cloud.
- ☐ Oracle Financial Cloud performs the financial transactions for the order. It creates an invoice, manages accounts receivable, processes payments, and manages revenue.

FUSION HCM

5.1 CORE HR SETUP

Introduction

Setup Starts with Understanding the Client's System Requirements and Mapping the same to the Fusion Application. Workforce Deployment (Core HR) Offering Setup Forms the Basis. Below are the Setup Steps

Create Implementation Users

Navigator: Setup and Maintenance → Tasks → Search → Create Implementation Users

Create an Implementation user and assign all the required roles.

Manage Geographies

Navigator: Setup and Maintenance → Tasks → Search → Manage Geographies

Manage Countries as per the Client's Requirements

Manage Legal Addresses

Navigator: Setup and Maintenance → Tasks → Search → Manage Legal Addresses

Create Locations and its complete Address details

Establish Enterprise Structures

Navigator: Setup and Maintenance → Tasks → Search → Establish Enterprise Structures

Enterprise Serves as a Top Organization Level and it's an Ultimate Holding Company.

Manage Enterprise HCM Information

Navigator: Setup and Maintenance → Tasks → Search → Manage Enterprise HCM Information

Here we manage the Enterprise Description, Other Classifications, Work Day Information, Enterprise Information, Currency Support Information, User and Role Provisioning Information, etc…

Manage Divisions

Navigator: Setup and Maintenance → Tasks → Search → Manage Divisions

Division is **Not Mandatory**, but Suggest the Client use Division as it will be useful for Financial Concept. In accounting, there is something called Balancing Segment. So, you can use Division and have it as a Balancing Segment in your Accounting Structure.

Whatever u can achieve through Division can also be achieved through Business Unit, but you cannot use BU as a qualified segment in your Accounting Structure.

Manage Legislative Data Groups

Navigator: Setup and Maintenance → Tasks → Search → Manage Legislative Data Groups

Legislative Data Group is a Classification which classifies Payroll related data Country Wise. LDG is **Mandatory**. For each country we must have one LDG, Only then we can hire the employees for the country and would be able to process the payroll

Manage Legal Entity

Navigator: Setup and Maintenance → Tasks → Search → Manage Legal Entity

Legal Entity is **Mandatory**, the Authorized Company (or) Registered Company Which is responsible for Hiring Employees. If the company has multiple Offices in different countries, each of the country offices needs to be created as separate legal entities. This is a stand-alone entity and no hierarchy supported here. Also, this is not linked to any other entity of the work structure

Manage Legal Entity HCM Information

Navigator: Setup and Maintenance → Tasks → Search → Manage Legal Entity HCM Information

Here we manage the Legal Entity HCM information

Manage Business Unit

Navigator: Setup and Maintenance → Tasks → Search → Manage Business Unit

Business Unit is **Mandatory**, the Individual Operations of the Company is mapped to the business units.

Manage Departments

Navigator: Setup and Maintenance → Tasks → Search → Manage Departments

Department is **Mandatory**, this is where people are actually working. The Cost Centers of the Company are defined as departments. You can define Costing Structure here and use the same for your payroll costing.

Manage Reference Data Sets

Navigator: Setup and Maintenance → Tasks → Search → Manage Reference Data Sets

Reference Data Set is for Security like, the Particular Grade should be Applicable to Employee hired in this Legal Entity. Let's say we have n number of Job, Grade, Locations, Departments and you want to secure, we use RDS. If I am hiring someone in Particular Business Unit, he should be assigned to only a particular Location (or) Department, here we use RDS.

Manage Locations

Navigator: Setup and Maintenance → Tasks → Search → Manage Locations

Here we manage Locations and Location basic details, Location information, Contact Details, Main Address, Shipping Details, etc…

Manage Grades

Navigator: Setup and Maintenance → Tasks → Search → Manage Grades

Here we manage grades, grades basic details, grade step details to be assigned to the employees

Manage Jobs

Navigator: Setup and Maintenance → Tasks → Search → Manage Jobs

Here we manage jobs, jobs basic details and valid grades of the job details.

Manage Positions

Navigator: Setup and Maintenance → Tasks → Search → Manage Positions

Here we manage positions, positions basic details and valid grades of the position details.

5.2 HCM DATA LOADER

Introduction

HCM Data Loader (HDL) is a tool for loading and maintaining data.

Supported Key Types

HDL Supports below Key Types

- ☐ 1. Oracle Fusion GUID
- ☐ 2. Oracle Fusion surrogate ID
- ☐ 3. Source Key
- ☐ 4. User Key

Oracle Fusion GUID & Oracle Fusion surrogate ID are generated automatically

Source Key is used to create and update business objects. Source Key has two Components.

- ☐ **SourceSystemOwner** – It is defined in **HRC_SOURCE_SYSTEM_OWNER** Lookup. It is used to identify where the data is originated.
- ☐ **SourceSystemId** – It must be unique and it is used in the source system

User Key is used to maintain an object that was not created with **Source Key**. Mostly, User Key is used to update business objects.

Below are few key HDL Templates of HCM Business Objects (for reference)

Grade.dat

```
METADATA|Grade|SourceSystemOwner|SourceSystemId|EffectiveStartDate|Effect
iveEndDate|SetCode|GradeCode|GradeName|ActiveStatus

MERGE|Grade|SourceSystemOwnerName|GRADE-
TEST_GRADE_1|1951/01/01|4712/12/31|COMMON|E18|E18|A
```

Location.dat

```
METADATA|Location|SourceSystemOwner|SourceSystemId|EffectiveStartDate|Eff
ectiveEndDate|LocationCode|LocationName|Description|SetCode|Country|Activ
eStatus|ShipToSiteFlag|ReceivingSiteFlag|BillToSiteFlag|OfficeSiteFlag|Bu
ilding|PostalCode|TownOrCity|Region1|Region2|AddressLine1

MERGE|Location|SourceSystemOwnerName|LOC-
TEST_1|1951/01/01|4712/12/31|DOY_PRA_Location|DOY_PRA_Location|DOY_PRA_Lo
cation|COMMON|US|A|Y|Y|Y|Y|Central Perks|10130|New York|New
York|NY|Central Perks Coffee Shop
```

Job.dat

```
METADATA|Job|SourceSystemOwner|SourceSystemId|EffectiveStartDate|Effectiv
eEndDate|SetCode|JobCode|Name|ActiveStatus|MedicalCheckupRequired|Benchma
rkJobFlag

MERGE|Job|SourceSystemOwnerName|JOB-
TEST_JOB_1|1951/01/01|4712/12/31|COMMON|ORA_CON|Oracle Consultant|A|N|N
```

Position.dat

```
METADATA|Position|SourceSystemOwner|SourceSystemId|EffectiveStartDate|Eff
ectiveEndDate|BusinessUnitName|PositionCode|Name|ActiveStatus|DepartmentN
ame|JobSetCode|JobCode|LocationCode|FullPartTime|RegularTemporary|HiringS
tatus|FTE|HeadCount|PositionType
```

```
MERGE|Position|SourceSystemOwnerName|POS-
TEST_POS_1|1951/01/01|4712/12/31|USA Business Unit 01|TEST_POS_1|Cloud
Applications Marketing|A|Cloud Applications -
US|COMMON|ORA_CON|DOY_PRA_Location|FULL_TIME|R|APPROVED|10|10|SHARED
```

Organization.dat

```
METADATA|Organization|SourceSystemOwner|SourceSystemId|Name|Classificatio
nCode|EffectiveStartDate|EffectiveEndDate|LocationId(SourceSystemId)|Loca
tionSetCode
```

```
MERGE|Organization|SourceSystemOwnerName|DEPT-TEST_DEPT_1|Cloud
Applications - Consultant|DEPARTMENT|1951/01/01|4712/12/31|LOC-
TEST_1|COMMON
```

```
METADATA|OrgUnitClassification|SourceSystemOwner|SourceSystemId|Effective
StartDate|EffectiveEndDate|OrganizationId(SourceSystemId)|ClassificationC
ode|SetCode|Status
```

```
MERGE|OrgUnitClassification|SourceSystemOwnerName|DEPT_CLS-
TEST_DEPT_1|1951/01/01|4712/12/31|DEPT-TEST_DEPT_1|DEPARTMENT|COMMON|A
```

Worker.dat

```
METADATA|Worker|SourceSystemOwner|SourceSystemId|EffectiveStartDate|Effec
tiveEndDate|PersonNumber|StartDate|DateOfBirth|ActionCode|BloodType|Count
ryOfBirth
```

```
MERGE|Worker|SourceSystemOwnerName|PER-
1|2017/01/01|4712/12/31|DOY_TEST_0001|2017/01/01|1984/08/08|HIRE|A+|US
```

```
METADATA|PersonName|SourceSystemOwner|SourceSystemId|PersonId(SourceSyste
mId)|PersonNumber|LegislationCode|NameType|LastName|FirstName|Title|Effec
tiveStartDate|EffectiveEndDate
```

```
MERGE|PersonName|SourceSystemOwnerName|PN-1|PER-
1|DOY_TEST_0001|US|GLOBAL|Nagarajan|Prathap|Mr.|2017/01/01|4712/12/31
```

```
METADATA|WorkRelationship|SourceSystemOwner|SourceSystemId|PersonId(Sourc
eSystemId)|PersonNumber|DateStart|LegalEmployerName|WorkerType|PrimaryFla
g|ActionCode
```

```
MERGE|WorkRelationship|SourceSystemOwnerName|WR-1|PER-
1|DOY_TEST_0001|2017/01/01|LegalEmployerName|E|Y|HIRE
```

```
METADATA|WorkTerms|SourceSystemOwner|SourceSystemId|AssignmentNumber|Peri
odOfServiceId(SourceSystemId)|EffectiveStartDate|EffectiveEndDate|Effecti
veSequence|EffectiveLatestChange|ActionCode|PersonId(SourceSystemId)|Pers
onNumber|LegalEmployerName|DateStart|WorkerType|BusinessUnitShortCode
```

```
MERGE|WorkTerms|SourceSystemOwnerName|WT-1|WT_DOY_TEST_0001|WR-
1|2017/01/01|4712/12/31|1|Y|HIRE|PER-
1|DOY_TEST_0001|LegalEmployerName|2017/01/01|E|USA Business Unit 01
```

```
METADATA|Assignment|SourceSystemOwner|SourceSystemId|AssignmentNumber|Wor
kTermsAssignmentId(SourceSystemId)|PersonId(SourceSystemId)|PersonNumber|
EffectiveStartDate|EffectiveEndDate|EffectiveSequence|EffectiveLatestChan
ge|DateStart|ActionCode|PersonTypeCode|LegalEmployerName|BusinessUnitShor
tCode|JobCode|GradeCode|DepartmentName|PositionCode|LocationCode|PrimaryA
ssignmentFlag|PrimaryFlag|ManagerFlag
```

```
MERGE|Assignment|SourceSystemOwnerName|ASG-1|ASS_DOY_TEST_0001|WT-1|PER-
1|DOY_TEST_0001|2017/01/01|4712/12/31|1|Y|2017/01/01|HIRE|Employee|LegalE
mployerName|USA    Business    Unit    01|ORA_CON|E18|Cloud   Applications   -
Consultant|TEST_POS_1|55|Y|Y|N
```

Salary.dat

```
METADATA|Salary|SourceSystemOwner|SourceSystemId|ActionCode|ActionReasonC
ode|AssignmentId(SourceSystemId)|DateFrom|DateTo|SalaryAmount|SalaryBasis
Name|MultipleComponents|SalaryApproved
```

```
MERGE|Salary|SourceSystemOwnerName|SAL-1|CHANGE_SALARY|CMP_NEWH|ASG-
1|2017/01/01|4712/12/31|7.25|US Hourly|N|Y
```

Importing and Data Loading using HDL

Follow these steps:

- ☐ Go to **Navigator →Data Exchange → Tasks →Import and Load Data**
- ☐ Select Import File →Import Local File.
- ☐ In the Select File dialog box, click Browse to search for and select your file (**.dat** file needs to be **ZIP**ped and selected).
- ☐ Click Submit to upload your file to the Oracle WebCenter Content server. The file is loaded automatically to the HCM Data Loader import account hcm/dataloader/import and allocated a unique content ID.
- ☐ File gets submitted as Data Set and HDL gets Processed

5.3 HCM EXTRACTS

Introduction

HCM Extracts is a tool commonly used for outbound integration. Reports and Data files are generated using HCM Extracts.

Below is the sequence to create an **HCM Extract**

- ☐ Create **Extract Definition and** Select/Add **Parameters**
- ☐ Create **Data Groups,** Connect **Data Groups** and add **Data Group Filter Criteria**
- ☐ Create **Records**
- ☐ Create **Extract Attributes**
- ☐ Add **Extract Delivery Options**

Extract Definition

Navigator: My Client Groups → Data Exchange → Manage Extract Definitions

Enter basic information of an Extract like Extract Name, Extract Type, Category, Legislative Data Group and Select/Add Parameters. Most Commonly used Parameters are Effective Date, Changes Only. Changes Only Parameter is used to extract while reporting the changes in extracting components.

Extract Type	Purpose
Full Profile	Use for complete employee and payroll data archives.
Payroll Interface	Use for providing data to third party payroll service providers.
Payments	Use for salary payment method archives. For example, Paid through check or bank transfer.
Benefit Carrier	Use for providing data to third party benefits service providers.

Archive Retrieval	Use for reports based on permanently archived data, for example, payslip.
EOY Archive	Use for end of year archives (HR, Benefits).
HR Archive	Use for all HR archives.
Payroll Archive	Use for all payroll or payslip archives.
Other Payroll Archive	Use for all payroll archives.

Source: Standard Documentation on HCM Extracts

Data Groups

Create Data Groups with information like User Entity, Threading Database Item, Root Data Group, Threading Action Type. Connect the Parent Data Groups with the Child Data Groups with Proper Database Items. Data Group Filter Criteria are used to filter the records as per the client's requirements.

User Entity – User Entities holds the Database items. Search and select for a user entity as per the client's requirements which holds the required data. Selecting any one of the Data Groups as Root Data Group is Mandatory. Commonly used User Entities are **PER_EXT_PAY_EMPLOYEES_UE, ELEMENT ENTRIES RANGE, PERSONAL_PAYMENTS_RANGE**

Threading Database Item – Threading database item is required for implementing the Changes Only feature. The threading database item is a unique ID in the chosen user entity. Generally, for the PER_EXT_PAY_EMPLOYEES_UE user entity, it would be **Extract Employee Assignment ID**.

Threading Action Type – Object Actions, Relationship Actions, Temporary Actions are Threading Action types available. Mostly we choose **Object Actions**

Records

Record is a Collection of Attributes in a required sequence. We can also select the next data group to identify which data group the application should process next. Each Data Group holds a Record and its corresponding attributes.

Attributes

Individual fields in Extract Records are called Attributes. Required Database items are referred to in the Attributes. Create all the required fields at the Attribute level.

For Changes only file, **Key Attribute, Mark as Changed, Exclude from Comparison, Always Display** fields Plays a key role. Select those fields as per the requirement.

If a Database item is not available for the required attribute, we can get it using **Extract Rule** Formula.

Note: To refer Extract Rule Formula, We need to select Type as Rule and Rule as the Custom Extract Rule Formula created.

Sample Extract Rule Formula

```
DEFAULT FOR DATA_ELEMENT_CODE IS ' '
DEFAULT FOR PER_PER_PERSON_NUMBER IS 'X'
DEFAULT FOR PER_ASG_ASSIGNMENT_NUMBER IS 'X'
DEFAULT FOR PER_LEGAL_EMPLOYER_NAME IS 'X'
DEFAULT FOR DATA_ELEMENTS IS EMPTY_TEXT_TEXT

INPUTS ARE DATA_ELEMENT_CODE (TEXT), DATA_ELEMENTS (TEXT_TEXT)

IF (DATA_ELEMENT_CODE = 'Attribute Tag Name') THEN
(
    L_LEGAL_EMPLOYER = DATA_ELEMENTS['Legal_Employer']
    L_COMPANY_CODE    =    GET_VALUE_SET    ('GET_ADP_COMPANY_CODE_VS',
'|=L_LEGAL_EMPLOYER='''|| L_LEGAL_EMPLOYER||'''')
    rule_value = L_COMPANY_CODE
)
ELSE
(
    rule_value = ' '
)

RETURN rule_value
```

Delivery Options

Mostly we create a BI Publisher report and refer it at the Delivery Options to get the output file in the required format. Below is a sample for reference.

Field	Value
Start Date	01/01/1951
End Date	12/31/4712
Delivery Option Name	Enter a name E.g., **Email to HR**
Output Type	As required E.g., **Text**
Report	Enter the BI Report Path E.g., **/Custom/Human Capital Management/HREmailReport.xdo**
Template Name	Enter the Exact BI Report Template Name
Output Name	Enter any Output Name E.g., **EmailtoHR.csv**
Delivery Type	As required E.g., **Email**

Once all the above steps are completed, compile All Formula & Validate at Extract Execution Tree level.

Submitting an Extract

- ☐ Go to **Navigator → Payroll Checklist → Tasks → Submit a Process or Report**
- ☐ Select **Legislative Data Group** & **HCM Extract Name** (Flow Pattern) and Click **Next**

☐ Enter a unique Payroll Flow Name and the required Parameters of Extract and Click **Submit**

(**or**)

☐ Go to **Navigator** → **My Client Groups** → **Data Exchange** → **Manage Extract Definitions**

☐ Select **HCM Extract Name** and Click **Submit Extracts**

☐ Enter a unique Extract Instance Name and the required Parameters of Extract and click **Submit**

5.4 PAYROLL BATCH LOADER

Introduction

Payroll Batch Loader (PBL) is used for bulk loading of objects using spreadsheets.

We are going to cover Payroll Batch Loader using

☐ Batch Loader Spreadsheet
☐ Transformation formula

Batch Loader Spreadsheet

In the below example, we are going to create element entries for Overtime earnings for an employee using the payroll batch loader.

Prerequisites

☐ Go to **Tools** → **Download Desktop Integration Installer** and install Oracle ADF Desktop Integration Add-In for Excel

☐ Create the Overtime element at the assignment level for element entries

☐ Identify the assignment numbers of the Employees who receive the overtime element entries

Creating a Batch Header

☐ Go to **Navigator** → **Payroll Administration** → **Tasks** → **Batch Loader**

☐ Download **Batch Loader Spreadsheet (DesktopGenericBatchLoader.xlsx)** and Open the file

- ☐ When prompted to connect, click Yes. Login with User ID and Password and then Click Sign In.
- ☐ Enter the Batch Name column and select the Legislative Data Group from the list and click Save.
- ☐ Click OK in the Upload Options dialog box. Now the batch is created and Row inserted successfully status gets displayed.

Creating Batch Content

- ☐ Double-click the batch name in the Batch Header Sheet and then navigate to the Batch Content Sheet.
- ☐ Click Add and select the task and task action as below:
  - o Enter Element Entry in the Task Name field.
  - o Enter Create Element Entry in the Task Action Name field.
  - o Enter the element name (E.g: Overtime) in the Reference field.
  - o Click Search and Select the required row and then click OK.
- ☐ Double-click the Create Element Entry task action name which generates the line for the Element with all Input Values.
- ☐ Enter all the required Input Values in the Batch Content Line Details. (Sample below)

Line Sequence	Effective Start Date	Person Number	Assignment Number	Overtime Hours
1	2019-09-01	12	E12	8

- ☐ Click Save and click OK in the Upload Options dialog box.

Transferring the Batch

- ☐ Go to **Navigator → Payroll Administration → Tasks → Submit a Process or Report**
- ☐ Select the Legislative Data Group and Select **Transfer Batch** Flow Pattern
- ☐ Enter a unique Payroll Flow name and select the Batch Name entered in the Batch Header sheet and click Submit.

☐ Element Entries for the corresponding Person numbers would have got created successfully.

Transformation Formula

In the below example, we are going to create element entries for Overtime earnings for an employee the same as above, but now using the **Transformation Formula**.

Transformation Formula could be used while **Automating** Payroll Batch Loader

Data File preparation

☐ Prepare a Data file **(.csv/.txt)** with required Input Values (Sample below)
   o **12,E12,2019-09-01,8**
☐ Then Go to **Navigator → Tools → File Import and Export** and Place the Data file in WCC
   o (For Automation Process, Files needs to be automatically sent to WCC with UNIQUE_NAME)

Batch Loader Formula

Write a **Batch Loader** type **Fast Formula** to match the Data File (Sample below)

```
/* Inputs   */
INPUTS ARE OPERATION (text)
,LINENO (number)
,LINESEQUENCE (number)
,LINEREPEATNO (number)
,POSITION1 (text)
,POSITION2 (text)
,POSITION3 (text)
,POSITION4 (text)

DEFAULT FOR LINENO       IS 1
DEFAULT FOR LINEREPEATNO IS 1
DEFAULT FOR LINESEQUENCE IS 1
DEFAULT FOR POSITION1    IS 'NO DATA'
DEFAULT FOR POSITION2    IS 'NO DATA'
DEFAULT FOR POSITION3    IS 'NO DATA'
DEFAULT FOR POSITION4    IS 'NO DATA'
```

```
/* Calculations */
IF OPERATION='FILETYPE' THEN
   OUTPUTVALUE='DELIMITED'
ELSE IF OPERATION='DELIMITER' THEN
   OUTPUTVALUE=','
ELSE IF OPERATION='READ' THEN
   OUTPUTVALUE='NONE'
ELSE IF OPERATION='MAP' THEN
(
   MESSAGE=' '
   MESSAGELEVEL=' '
   LC_ERROR_FLAG='N'
   SUPPRESSINVALIDPARAMETER = 'Y'
   LC_DATE_FORMAT='YYYY-MM-DD'
   EFFECTIVE_END_DATE='4712-12-31'
   ACTIONREFERENCE       = ' '
   ELEMENT               = ' '

   /*Batch Related Outputs*/
   TASK='Element Entry'

   L_PERSON_NUMBER          = Trim(POSITION1)
   L_ASSIGNMENT_NUMBER      = Trim(POSITION2)
   L_EFFECTIVE_START_DATE   = Trim(POSITION3)
   HOURS                    = Trim(POSITION4)
   LC_ELEMENT_NAME          = 'Overtime'

   IF ISNULL(L_ASSIGNMENT_NUMBER) = 'Y' THEN
   (

   TASK                   ='Element Entry'
   LC_TASKACTION_CREATE_EE ='Create Element Entry'
   LC_TASKACTION_UPDATE_EE ='Update Element Entry'
   PERSON_NUMBER          = L_PERSON_NUMBER
   ASSIGNMENT_NUMBER      = L_ASSIGNMENT_NUMBER
   EFFECTIVE_AS_OF_DATE   = L_EFFECTIVE_START_DATE
   EFFECTIVE_START_DATE   = L_EFFECTIVE_START_DATE
```

```
    ACTIONREFERENCE            = LC_ELEMENT_NAME
    ELEMENT                    = LC_ELEMENT_NAME
    /* To Check whether the element entry already exists (to
understand update)*/
    LC_ELEMENT_ENTRY_CHECK                                    =
GET_VALUE_SET('XXX_ELEMENT_ENTRY_CHECK','|=P_ASSIGNMENT_NUMBER='''
||L_ASSIGNMENT_NUMBER||''''||
'|P_ELEMENT_NAME='''||LC_ELEMENT_NAME||''''||
'|P_EFFECTIVE_DATE='''||L_EFFECTIVE_START_DATE||'''')

    IF LC_ELEMENT_ENTRY_CHECK = 'Y' THEN
    (
    TASKACTION=LC_TASKACTION_UPDATE_EE
    )
    ELSE
    (
    TASKACTION=LC_TASKACTION_CREATE_EE
    )

      IF TASKACTION=LC_TASKACTION_CREATE_EE THEN
      (
        RETURN
TASK,TASKACTION,LINESEQUENCE,ACTIONREFERENCE,SUPPRESSINVALIDPARAME
TER,EFFECTIVE_START_DATE,EFFECTIVE_END_DATE,PERSON_NUMBER,ASSIGNME
NT_NUMBER,HOURS,MESSAGE,MESSAGELEVEL
      )
      IF TASKACTION=LC_TASKACTION_UPDATE_EE THEN
      (
        RETURN
TASK,TASKACTION,LINESEQUENCE,ACTIONREFERENCE,EFFECTIVE_AS_OF_DATE,
PERSON_NUMBER,ASSIGNMENT_NUMBER,HOURS,MESSAGE,MESSAGELEVEL
      )


      )
ELSE
      (
LC_ERROR_FLAG = 'Y'

IF LC_ERROR_FLAG = 'Y' THEN
```

```
       (
TASKACTION='Create Element Entry'
ACTIONREFERENCE = 'Error Processing'
MESSAGELEVEL='F'
File_Type = 'Overtime Hours File'
File_Line  =  SUBSTR('Given  employment  record  cannot  be  found.
'||POSITION1,1,240)
Line_Sequence = LINESEQUENCE
MESSAGE    =    Substr(MESSAGE  +  '  ~  LINESEQUENCE  '  +
To_Char(LINESEQUENCE) + ' ~ File Line ~ ' + File_Line ,1,4000)
Error_Message = MESSAGE
Error_Type = 'Message Level ' + MESSAGELEVEL
RETURN
TASK,TASKACTION,LINESEQUENCE,ACTIONREFERENCE,MESSAGE,MESSAGELEVEL,
File_Type,File_Line,Line_Sequence,Error_Message,Error_Type
       )
)

)
ELSE
    OUTPUTVALUE='NONE'
RETURN OUTPUTVALUE
/* End Formula Text */
```

Creating Payroll Flow for Loading and Transferring Batch

- ☐ Go to **Navigator → Payroll Checklist → Tasks → Manage Payroll Flow Patterns**
- ☐ Create a Custom Flow Pattern copying Seeded Load and Transfer Batch Flow Pattern
- ☐ Update the **Load Batch Task Details: Basic Information** of the Custom Flow Pattern as below :

Name	Parameter Basis	Basis Value	Hint
Batch	Post SQL Bind	SELECT 'UNIQUE_BATCH' FROM DUAL	Query to get unique Batch

Batch Name	Post SQL Bind	SELECT 'UNIQUE_BATCH_NAME' FROM DUAL	Query to get unique Batch Name
Content Id	Post SQL Bind	SELECT MAX(ddocname) FROM revisions WHERE did IN (SELECT did FROM revisions WHERE ddoctitle LIKE 'UNIQUE_NAME'|| (SELECT TO_CHAR (SYSDATE, 'DD-MM-YYYY') || '%' FROM DUAL)) AND TRUNC(DCREATEDATE) = TRUNC(SYSDATE) AND ddocname LIKE 'UNIQUE_NAME%'	Query to pick the exact file to be processed from WCC
Transformation Formula	Post SQL Bind	select max(formula_id) from ff_formulas_vl ff, ff_formula_types ft where ff.formula_type_id = ft.formula_type_id and ft.formula_type_name = 'Batch Loader' and ff.formula_name = 'BATCH_LOADER_FORMULA_ NAME'	Query to map the Batch Loader Formula Created

☐ Scheduling the Custom Flow Pattern automates the Element Entry Creation.

5.5 ABSENCE MANAGEMENT SETUP

Introduction

Below is the Setup Sequence for Absence Management.

Manage Work Shifts

Navigator: Setup and Maintenance → Tasks → Search → Manage Work Shifts

Here we create the Shift (Time/Duration/Elapsed) and its Category, Start Time, Shift Detail Type and the Duration

Manage Work Workday Patterns

Navigator: Setup and Maintenance → Tasks → Search → Manage Work Workday Patterns

Here we create the Work Workday Pattern and associate the work shift and other details like Length in days, Start Day and End Day

Manage Work Schedules

Navigator: Setup and Maintenance → Tasks → Search → Manage Work Schedules

Here we create the Work Schedule and associate the Work Pattern and other details like Exceptions and Eligibility Profiles details

Manage Work Schedule Assignment Administration

Navigator: Setup and Maintenance → Tasks → Search → Manage Work Schedule Assignment Administration

This decides at which Level Work Schedule has to be assigned. **Levels** could be Enterprise, Legal Employer, Department, Employment Terms, Assignment, Location, Job or Position

Manage Geography Trees

Navigator: Setup and Maintenance → Tasks → Search → Manage Geography Trees

This Setup is done at Country Level or Location Level. Create it, Set Status as Active, Online Audit it and Flatten it (Row/Column)

Manage Calendar Events

Navigator: Setup and Maintenance → Tasks → Search → Manage Calendar Events

This is the Place where we define Public Holidays & Assign under the Created Geography

Manage Eligibility Profiles

Navigator: Setup and Maintenance → Tasks → Search → Manage Eligibility Profiles

This is the Place where we restrict the absence types (or) absence plans to certain criteria.

Manage Derived Factors

Navigator: Setup and Maintenance → Tasks → Search → Manage Derived Factors

Here we manage Age, Length of Service, Compensation, Hours worked Derived Factors. Length of Service is a majorly-used Derived Factor.

Manage Absence Reasons

Navigator: Setup and Maintenance → Tasks → Search → Manage Absence Reasons

Absence Reason is a Supplemental description of the function or cause of an absence. For each Absence Type, we can associate Absence reasons and validation can be done.

Manage Absence Certifications

Navigator: Setup and Maintenance → Tasks → Search → Manage Absence Certifications

For some Absence Types, we can associate Absence Certifications where we define Absence Record Update Rule, Trigger, Due Date Rule and other validation Action details like On Creation, On Passage of Due Date and On Completion.

Manage Repeating Time Periods

Navigator: Setup and Maintenance → Tasks → Search → Manage Repeating Time Periods

The accrual processing frequency will depend on the Repeating Time Period. This is the Place where we define how the Accrual Frequency Like Daily, Monthly, Yearly, etc...

Manage Absence Plans

Navigator: Setup and Maintenance → Tasks → Search → Manage Absence Plans

Absence Plan is a Compensation Offering that describes if and how to pay for absences. There are three Absence Plan Types. They are **Accrual, Qualification, No Entitlement.**

Accrual is the Plan type where the days of absence get accrued. We use this type for Absence types like Annual Leave, Privilege Leave. Here we define Plan Terms, Enrollment Rules, Termination Rules, Eligibility, Accrual Attributes, Plan Limits, Accrual Matrix, Balance Updates, Rates and Payroll Integration details.

Qualification is the Plan type used for Absence types like Sick Leave, Maternity Leave. Here we define Plan Terms, Enrollment Rules, Eligibility, Entitlement Attributes, Qualification Band Matrix, Qualification Details, Rates and Payroll Integration details.

No Entitlement is the Plan type used for Unpaid Leaves. Here we define Plan Terms, Enrollment Rules, Balance Disposition Rules, Eligibility, Balance Updates, Rates and Payroll Integration details.

Manage Absence Types

Navigator: Setup and Maintenance → Tasks → Search → Manage Absence Types

Absence Type is the primary description of the absence. Absence Plans and Absence Reasons are associated to the Absence Type.

5.6 FAST FORMULAS

Introduction

Fast Formula is a tool to write formulas with basic mathematical functions. Fast formulas are expressions of calculations or comparisons with different input variables. Fast Formulas are used in performing functions like **Payroll Calculations, Absence Duration Calculation, Validating Element Inputs, Element Skip,** etc.

Fast Formulas are written in below sequence:

- ☐ ALIAS
- ☐ DEFAULT
- ☐ INPUTS
- ☐ CALCULATION
- ☐ RETURN

ALIAS

ALIAS is Optional. Alias is used for Database Items and Global Values.

Syntax: ALIAS VARIABLE1 AS VARIABLE2

DEFAULT

DEFAULT is used to default Database Items and Input Values. Fast Formula uses the Default Value when Database Items or Input Values Alias is NULL while running Formula for Database Items and Global Values.

Syntax: DEFAULT FOR VARIABLE_NAME IS VALUE

INPUTS

INPUTS are used to pass Input Values from the Element to the Formula. **DATE, TEXT, NUMBER** are the Datatypes.

Syntax: INPUTS ARE VARIABLE1 (DATATYPE), VARIABLE2 (DATATYPE)

CALCULATION

CALCULATION is an expression used to achieve the formula result as expected.

RETURN

RETURN is used to return the Output of the Calculation Process

FUNCTIONS used in Formula

ABS, FLOOR, GREATEST, LEAST, ROUND, ROUNDUP, TRUNC are the few Numeric Functions that can be used in Formula.

ADD_DAYS, ADD_MONTHS, ADD_YEAR, GREATEST, LEAST, DAYS_BETWEEN, MONTHS_BETWEEN are the few Date Functions that can be used in Formula.

TO_CHAR, TO_DATE, TO_NUMBER, TO_TEXT are the few Data Functions that can be used in Formula.

GREATEST, LEAST, LENGTH, SUBSTRING, UPPER are the few Text Functions that can be used in Formula.

Types of Formula

There are different types of Formulas. In Oracle Fusion, Few commonly used formulas are **Oracle Payroll, Element Input Validation, Element Skip, Extract Rule,**

NAVIGATION

Navigator: Setup and Maintenance → Tasks → Search → Manage Fast Formulas

Above is the Navigation where we create Fast Formulas

Calling a Formula from another Formula

We can call a Fast Formula from another Formula.

Example:

```
DEFAULT FOR ASG_HR_ASG_ID     IS 0
DEFAULT FOR PAY_EARN_PERIOD_END IS '4712/12/31 00:00:00' (DATE)

SET_INPUT('HR_ASSIGNMENT_ID',ASG_HR_ASG_ID)
V_ASG_ID = ASG_HR_ASG_ID

L_DATE_EARNED = GET_CONTEXT(DATE_EARNED, PAY_EARN_PERIOD_END)

 CALL_FORMULA('GET_HR_DATA'
    ,ASG_HR_ASG_ID > 'HR_ID'
    ,L_DATE_EARNED > 'EFF_DATE'
    ,'PER_JOB_ATTRIBUTE1' > 'MODE'
    ,L_OUTPUT_TEXT < 'X_OUTPUT_TEXT' DEFAULT ' ')

V_JOB_ATT = L_OUTPUT_TEXT

RETURN V_JOB_ATT
```

Using Value Set in Formula

Value Sets can be called in Fast Formula.

Example:

```
INPUTS ARE HR_ID (NUMBER),
EFF_ST_DATE(TEXT),
EFF_END_DATE(TEXT),
MODE (TEXT)

L_HR_PER_ID   = HR_ID
L_EFF_ST_DATE = EFF_ST_DATE
L_EFF_END_DATE = EFF_END_DATE

X_OUTPUT     = '0001/01/01 00:00:00'  (DATE)
X_OUTPUT_NUMBER  = 0
X_OUTPUT_TEXT  = ' '

IF MODE = 'GROSS' THEN
(
    X_OUTPUT_TEXT  =  GET_VALUE_SET ('GET_GROSS_YTD_VALUE' ,
'|=L_PERSON_ID='''|| TO_CHAR(L_HR_PER_ID)||''''||'|L_CMP_START_DATE='''||
L_EFF_ST_DATE ||''''||'|L_CMP_END_DATE='''|| L_EFF_END_DATE ||'''')
)
ELSE
(
    X_OUTPUT_TEXT  =  '0'
)

RETURN X_OUTPUT_TEXT
```

Sample Formulas

Below are the Sample Formulas which would be helpful for creating Formulas as per the Client's requirement.

Element Input Validation

Element Input Validation formula is used to validate element entry values.

```
DEFAULT FOR ENTRY_VALUE IS 0
INPUTS ARE ENTRY_VALUE
IF ENTRY_VALUE>10 THEN
(
FORMULA_MESSAGE='The amount is invalid, enter an amount less than $10'
```

```
FORMULA_STATUS='E'
)

RETURN FORMULA_STATUS, FORMULA_MESSAGE
```

Element Skip

Element Skip formula is used to Skip the element entry to get Processed.

```
DEFAULT FOR PAY_EARN_PERIOD_END IS '0001/01/01 00:00:00' (date)
DEFAULT FOR SKIP_FLAG IS 'Y'

IF TO_CHAR (TRUNC (PAY_EARN_PERIOD_END,'MON'),'MON') = 'APR' THEN
    SKIP_FLAG = 'Y'
ELSE
    SKIP_FLAG = 'N'
RETURN SKIP_FLAG
```

Extract Rule

Element Rule formula is used in HCM Extracts to return Non-Database Items.

```
DEFAULT FOR DATA_ELEMENT_CODE IS ' '
DEFAULT FOR PER_PER_PERSON_NUMBER IS 'X'
DEFAULT FOR PER_ASG_ASSIGNMENT_NUMBER IS 'X'
DEFAULT FOR PER_LEGAL_EMPLOYER_NAME IS 'X'
DEFAULT FOR DATA_ELEMENTS IS EMPTY_TEXT_TEXT

INPUTS ARE DATA_ELEMENT_CODE (TEXT), DATA_ELEMENTS (TEXT_TEXT)

IF (DATA_ELEMENT_CODE = 'Company_Code') THEN
(
    L_LEGAL_EMPLOYER = DATA_ELEMENTS['Legal_Employer']
    L_COMPANY_CODE = GET_VALUE_SET ( 'GET_COMPANY_CODE_VS' ,
'|=L_LEGAL_EMPLOYER='''|| L_LEGAL_EMPLOYER||'''')
    RULE_VALUE = L_COMPANY_CODE
)
ELSE IF (DATA_ELEMENT_CODE = 'Deduction_Code') THEN
(
    L_ELEMENT_NAME  = DATA_ELEMENTS['Element_Name']
    L_DEDUCTION_CODE = GET_VALUE_SET ( 'GET_DEDUCTION_CODE_VS' ,
'|=L_ELEMENT_NAME='''|| L_ELEMENT_NAME||'''')
    RULE_VALUE = L_DEDUCTION_CODE
)
ELSE
(
```

```
    RULE_VALUE = ' '
)

RETURN RULE_VALUE
```

Payroll Access to HR

In Some Formula Types, We can get HR Data directly. To get HR Data in such Formulas, Payroll Access to HR Formula is called to get such data.

```
DEFAULT FOR PER_ASG_GRADE_ID IS -1
DEFAULT FOR PER_ASG_PERSON_ID IS -1
DEFAULT FOR PER_ASG_GRADE_ATTRIBUTE_NUMBER1 IS 0
DEFAULT FOR PER_ASG_ATTRIBUTE_NUMBER2 IS 0

INPUTS ARE HR_ID (NUMBER),
           EFF_DATE(DATE),
           MODE (TEXT)

L_HR_ASS_ID   = HR_ID
L_HR_PER_ID   = HR_ID
L_EFF_DATE = EFF_DATE

X_OUTPUT      = '0001/01/01 00:00:00'  (DATE)
X_OUTPUT_NUMBER  = 0
X_OUTPUT_TEXT = ' '

IF MODE = 'GRADE_BONUS_PERCENT' THEN
(
   CHANGE_CONTEXTS (EFFECTIVE_DATE = L_EFF_DATE,HR_ASSIGNMENT_ID =
L_HR_ASS_ID)
   (
    X_OUTPUT_NUMBER  =  PER_ASG_GRADE_ATTRIBUTE_NUMBER1
   )
)
ELSE IF MODE = 'ASG_BONUS_PERCENT' THEN
(
   CHANGE_CONTEXTS (EFFECTIVE_DATE = L_EFF_DATE,HR_ASSIGNMENT_ID =
L_HR_ASS_ID)
   (
    X_OUTPUT_NUMBER  =  PER_ASG_ATTRIBUTE_NUMBER2
   )
)

RETURN X_OUTPUT_TEXT, X_OUTPUT_NUMBER
```

Compensation Default and Override

```
/*=========== DATABASE ITEM DEFAULTS BEGIN =====================*/
DEFAULT FOR CMP_IV_PLAN_START_DATE IS '2001/01/01'
DEFAULT FOR CMP_IV_PLAN_END_DATE IS '4012/01/01'
DEFAULT_DATA_VALUE FOR PER_HIST_ASG_ASSIGNMENT_ID IS 0
DEFAULT_DATA_VALUE FOR PER_HIST_ASG_ASSIGNMENT_TYPE IS 'x'
DEFAULT_DATA_VALUE FOR PER_HIST_ASG_ACTION_CODE IS 'x'
DEFAULT_DATA_VALUE FOR PER_HIST_ASG_EFFECTIVE_START_DATE IS '1900/01/01
00:00:00' (DATE)
DEFAULT_DATA_VALUE FOR PER_HIST_ASG_EFFECTIVE_END_DATE IS '4712/12/31
00:00:00' (DATE)
DEFAULT_DATA_VALUE FOR PER_HIST_ASG_PRIMARY_FLAG IS 'x'
DEFAULT FOR PER_ASG_ASSIGNMENT_ID IS 1
DEFAULT FOR PER_ASG_PERSON_ID IS 1
/*=========== DATABASE ITEM DEFAULTS END =====================*/

INPUTS ARE CMP_IV_PLAN_START_DATE (TEXT), CMP_IV_PLAN_END_DATE (TEXT)

/*=========== INITIALIZE THE VARIABLES BEGINS==================*/
L_DATA_TYPE = 'CHAR'
L_DEFAULT_VALUE = TO_CHAR(0)
L_BONUS_PRO = 0
/*=========== INITIALIZE THE VARIABLES ENDS=====================*/

L_PL_START_DATE = TO_DATE(CMP_IV_PLAN_START_DATE,'YYYY/MM/DD')
L_PL_END_DATE = TO_DATE(CMP_IV_PLAN_END_DATE,'YYYY/MM/DD')
L_PERD_ST_DATE = TO_DATE(CMP_IV_PLAN_START_DATE,'YYYY/MM/DD')
L_PERD_END_DATE = TO_DATE(CMP_IV_PLAN_END_DATE,'YYYY/MM/DD')

/*================ FORMULA SECTION BEGIN =====================*/
CHANGE_CONTEXTS(EFFECTIVE_DATE = L_PERD_END_DATE)
(
V_ASG_ID = PER_ASG_ASSIGNMENT_ID
V_PERSON_ID = PER_ASG_PERSON_ID
)

I =PER_HIST_ASG_ASSIGNMENT_ID.FIRST(-1)

WHILE PER_HIST_ASG_ASSIGNMENT_ID.EXISTS(I) LOOP
(

IF PER_HIST_ASG_PERSON_ID[I] = V_PERSON_ID AND
PER_HIST_ASG_ACTION_CODE[I] <> 'LOA' AND
```

```
PER_HIST_ASG_STATUS_TYPE[i]='ACTIVE' AND PER_HIST_ASG_PRIMARY_FLAG[i]='Y'
THEN
(

LC_ENTRY_CHECK =
GET_VALUE_SET('BONUS_PRORATION_DATE_CHECK_VS','|=P_PERSON_ID='''||TO_CHAR
(V_PERSON_ID)||''''||

'|P_PERIOD_START_DATE='''||TO_CHAR(L_PERD_ST_DATE,'YYYY-MM-DD')||''''||

'|P_PERIOD_END_DATE='''||TO_CHAR(L_PERD_END_DATE,'YYYY-MM-DD')||''''||

'|P_EFFECTIVE_START_DATE='''||TO_CHAR(PER_HIST_ASG_EFFECTIVE_START_DATE[I
],'YYYY-MM-DD')||''''||

'|P_EFFECTIVE_END_DATE='''||TO_CHAR(PER_HIST_ASG_EFFECTIVE_END_DATE[I],'Y
YYY-MM-DD')||'''')

IF LC_ENTRY_CHECK = 'Y' THEN
(

L_HIST_ASSIGNMENT_TYPE = PER_HIST_ASG_ASSIGNMENT_TYPE[I]
L_HIST_ASG_START_DATE  = PER_HIST_ASG_EFFECTIVE_START_DATE[I]
L_HIST_ASG_END_DATE    = PER_HIST_ASG_EFFECTIVE_END_DATE[I]

IF L_HIST_ASG_START_DATE < L_PERD_ST_DATE THEN
(
L_HIST_ASG_START_DATE = L_PERD_ST_DATE
)

IF L_HIST_ASG_END_DATE > L_PERD_END_DATE THEN
(
L_HIST_ASG_END_DATE = L_PERD_END_DATE
)

L_HIST_ASG_PRIMARY_FLAG = PER_HIST_ASG_PRIMARY_FLAG[I]
L_HIST_WR_PRIMARY_FLAG  = PER_HIST_ASG_PRIMARY_WORK_REL_FLAG[I]
L_HIST_ASG_STATUS_TYPE  = PER_HIST_ASG_STATUS_TYPE[I]

L_EVALUATION_PERIOD = DAYS_BETWEEN(L_PERD_END_DATE, L_PERD_ST_DATE)+1

IF L_HIST_ASG_START_DATE <> L_HIST_ASG_END_DATE THEN
(
CHANGE_CONTEXTS(EFFECTIVE_DATE = L_HIST_ASG_START_DATE)
(
```

```
 L_BONUS_PRO = L_BONUS_PRO + (((TRUNC(DAYS_BETWEEN(L_HIST_ASG_END_DATE,
L_HIST_ASG_START_DATE)+1))/L_EVALUATION_PERIOD))
)
)
)
)

I = PER_HIST_ASG_ASSIGNMENT_ID.NEXT(I,-1)
)

L_DEFAULT_VALUE = TO_CHAR(ROUND(L_BONUS_PRO,5))

RETURN  L_DATA_TYPE,L_DEFAULT_VALUE
```

Employment Seniority Date Adjustment

```
DEFAULT FOR SENIORITY_ADJUST_COMMENT IS 'no adjustment'
DEFAULT FOR SENIORITY_ADJUST_IN_DAYS IS 0
DEFAULT FOR SENIORITY_ADJUST_IN_HOURS IS 0
DEFAULT FOR CUMULATIVE_FLAG IS 'N'
DEFAULT FOR SENIORITY_BASIS IS 'ORA_PER_SNDT_DAYS'
DEFAULT FOR PER_PERSON_ENTERPRISE_HIRE_DATE IS '1900/01/01' (DATE)
DEFAULT FOR PREVIOUS_SENIORITY_EXIT_DATE is '1900/01/01 00:00:00' (DATE)
DEFAULT FOR BASE_SENIORITY_DATE is '1900/01/01 00:00:00' (DATE)
DEFAULT_DATA_VALUE FOR PER_HIST_ASG_PERSON_ID IS 0
DEFAULT_DATA_VALUE FOR PER_HIST_ASG_ASSIGNMENT_ID IS 0
DEFAULT_DATA_VALUE FOR PER_HIST_ASG_EFFECTIVE_START_DATE IS '1900/01/01
00:00:00' (DATE)
DEFAULT_DATA_VALUE FOR PER_HIST_ASG_EFFECTIVE_END_DATE IS '1900/01/01
00:00:00' (DATE)
DEFAULT_DATA_VALUE FOR PER_HIST_ASG_ASSIGNMENT_TYPE IS 'E'
DEFAULT_DATA_VALUE FOR PER_HIST_ASG_PRIMARY_FLAG IS 'Y'
DEFAULT_DATA_VALUE FOR PER_HIST_ASG_STATUS_TYPE IS 'X'
DEFAULT_DATA_VALUE FOR PER_HIST_ASG_ACTION_CODE IS 'X'
DEFAULT_DATA_VALUE FOR PER_HIST_ASG_USER_PERSON_TYPE IS 'X'

INPUTS ARE EFFECTIVE_START_DATE(DATE),
EFFECTIVE_END_DATE (DATE),
BASE_SENIORITY_DATE (DATE),
PREVIOUS_SENIORITY_EXIT_DATE (DATE),
SENIORITY_ADJUST_COMMENT(TEXT),
SENIORITY_ADJUST_IN_DAYS (NUMBER),
SENIORITY_ADJUST_IN_HOURS (NUMBER),
AUTO_ADJUSTMENT_DAYS (NUMBER)
```

```
L_ASG_ID = GET_CONTEXT(HR_ASSIGNMENT_ID, 0)
L_DATA = ESS_LOG_WRITE('L_ASG_ID => '+ TO_CHAR(L_ASG_ID))
L_PERSON_ID = GET_CONTEXT(PERSON_ID, 0)
L_DATA = ESS_LOG_WRITE('L_PERSON_ID => '+ TO_CHAR(L_PERSON_ID))
L_EFF_START_DATE = get_current_date()
L_EFF_END_DATE = '4712/12/31' (DATE)
L_INFINITY_DATE = '4712/12/31' (DATE)
ContextEffectiveDate = GET_CONTEXT(EFFECTIVE_DATE,'1900/01/01'(date))


EFF_DATE = EFFECTIVE_START_DATE
L_DAYS = 0
i = 1



change_contexts(EFFECTIVE_DATE = ContextEffectiveDate)
(
   WHILE  PER_HIST_ASG_ASSIGNMENT_ID.EXISTS(I) LOOP
    (
      IF PER_HIST_ASG_PERSON_ID[i]= L_PERSON_ID AND
PER_HIST_ASG_ASSIGNMENT_TYPE[i]= 'E' AND PER_HIST_ASG_PRIMARY_FLAG[i]='Y'
      AND PER_HIST_ASG_STATUS_TYPE[i]='ACTIVE' AND
PER_HIST_ASG_EFFECTIVE_START_DATE[i] = EFF_DATE THEN
          (

SENIORITY_HIRE_DATE = PER_PERSON_ENTERPRISE_HIRE_DATE

IF L_LATEST_HIRE_DATE > SENIORITY_HIRE_DATE THEN
(
SENIORITY_HIRE_DATE = L_LATEST_HIRE_DATE
)
ELSE
(
SENIORITY_HIRE_DATE = PER_PERSON_ENTERPRISE_HIRE_DATE
)

IF PER_HIST_ASG_EFFECTIVE_START_DATE[i] <> SENIORITY_HIRE_DATE THEN
(
L_EFF_START_DATE = SENIORITY_HIRE_DATE
)
ELSE
(
L_EFF_START_DATE = PER_HIST_ASG_EFFECTIVE_START_DATE[i]
)
```

```
IF PER_HIST_ASG_ACTION_CODE[i] = '102' OR PER_HIST_ASG_ACTION_CODE[i]
='GLB_TRANSFER' THEN
              (
              L_DAYS = DAYS_BETWEEN(PER_HIST_ASG_EFFECTIVE_START_DATE[i],
L_EFF_START_DATE)
)
ELSE
(
L_DAYS = 0
)
)


    i = i+1
   )
)


  SENIORITY_ADJUST_IN_DAYS = L_DAYS

return EFF_DATE, SENIORITY_ADJUST_COMMENT, SENIORITY_ADJUST_IN_DAYS,
SENIORITY_ADJUST_IN_HOURS
```

Participation and Rate Eligibility

```
/*=========== DATABASE ITEM DEFAULTS BEGIN ====================*/
DEFAULT_DATA_VALUE FOR PER_HIST_ASG_ASSIGNMENT_ID IS 0
DEFAULT_DATA_VALUE FOR PER_HIST_ASG_PERSON_ID IS 0
DEFAULT_DATA_VALUE FOR PER_HIST_ASG_POS_ID IS 0
DEFAULT_DATA_VALUE FOR PER_HIST_ASG_ASSIGNMENT_TYPE IS 'x'
DEFAULT_DATA_VALUE FOR PER_HIST_ASG_EFFECTIVE_START_DATE IS '1900/01/01
00:00:00' (DATE)
DEFAULT_DATA_VALUE FOR PER_HIST_ASG_EFFECTIVE_END_DATE IS '4712/12/31
00:00:00' (DATE)
DEFAULT_DATA_VALUE FOR PER_HIST_ASG_PRIMARY_FLAG IS 'x'
DEFAULT_DATA_VALUE FOR PER_HIST_ASG_PRIMARY_WORK_REL_FLAG IS 'x'
DEFAULT_DATA_VALUE FOR PER_HIST_ASG_USER_PERSON_TYPE IS 'x'
DEFAULT FOR PER_ASG_POSITION_ID IS -1
/*=========== DATABASE ITEM DEFAULTS END ====================*/

ELIGIBLE = 'N'
L_DATA_TYPE = 'CHAR'
L_DEFAULT_VALUE = TO_CHAR(0)
L_EFF_DATE = GET_CONTEXT(EFFECTIVE_DATE,'4712/12/31 00:00:00' (date))
/*L_EFF_DATE = get_current_date()*/
L_EFF_END_DATE = '4712/12/31 00:00:00' (date)
L_ASG_ID = GET_CONTEXT(HR_ASSIGNMENT_ID,-1)
```

```
L_PERSON_ID = GET_CONTEXT(PERSON_ID,-1)
L_MONTHS = 0

CHANGE_CONTEXTS(EFFECTIVE_DATE = L_EFF_DATE)
(
L_POSITION_ID = PER_ASG_POSITION_ID
)


I =PER_HIST_ASG_ASSIGNMENT_ID.FIRST(-1)

WHILE PER_HIST_ASG_ASSIGNMENT_ID.EXISTS(I) LOOP
(
L_HIST_PERSON_ID        = PER_HIST_ASG_PERSON_ID[I]
L_HIST_ASG_ID           = PER_HIST_ASG_ASSIGNMENT_ID[I]
L_HIST_POSITION_ID      = PER_HIST_ASG_POS_ID[I]
L_HIST_ASSIGNMENT_TYPE  = PER_HIST_ASG_ASSIGNMENT_TYPE[I]
L_HIST_ASG_START_DATE   = PER_HIST_ASG_EFFECTIVE_START_DATE[I]
L_HIST_ASG_END_DATE     = PER_HIST_ASG_EFFECTIVE_END_DATE[I]
L_HIST_ASG_PRIMARY_FLAG = PER_HIST_ASG_PRIMARY_FLAG[I]
L_HIST_WR_PRIMARY_FLAG  = PER_HIST_ASG_PRIMARY_WORK_REL_FLAG[I]
L_HIST_USER_PERSON_TYPE = PER_HIST_ASG_USER_PERSON_TYPE[I]
L_HIST_ASG_STATUS_TYPE  = PER_HIST_ASG_STATUS_TYPE[I]

IF ( L_ASG_ID = L_HIST_ASG_ID AND L_POSITION_ID = L_HIST_POSITION_ID AND
L_HIST_ASG_PRIMARY_FLAG = 'Y' AND L_HIST_WR_PRIMARY_FLAG = 'Y' AND
L_HIST_ASSIGNMENT_TYPE = 'E') THEN
(
L_ASG_START_DATE = L_HIST_ASG_START_DATE

IF L_EFF_DATE > L_HIST_ASG_END_DATE THEN
(
L_ASG_END_DATE   = L_HIST_ASG_END_DATE
)
ELSE
(
L_ASG_END_DATE   = L_EFF_DATE
)

CHANGE_CONTEXTS(EFFECTIVE_DATE = L_ASG_START_DATE)
(
 L_MONTHS = L_MONTHS + (((TRUNC(DAYS_BETWEEN(L_ASG_END_DATE,
L_ASG_START_DATE)+1))/365))*12
)
)
```

```
ELSE
(
L_MONTHS = 0
)

I = PER_HIST_ASG_ASSIGNMENT_ID.NEXT(I,-1)
)

L_DATA = ESS_LOG_WRITE('Months =>  '+ to_char(L_MONTHS))

IF L_MONTHS < 6 THEN
(
ELIGIBLE = 'Y'
)

RETURN ELIGIBLE
```

5.7 FUSION PAYROLL SETUP

Introduction

Below are the Setup Steps for Fusion Payroll.

Manage Organization Payment Methods

Navigator: Setup and Maintenance → Tasks → Search → Manage Organization Payment Methods

Here we manage the Organization Payment Methods like Check, Direct Deposit, International Transfer with its Payment Information, Payment Sources and Payment Method Rules.

Manage Personal Payment Methods

Navigator: My Client Groups → Person Management (Enter Person Number) → Tasks → Manage Personal Payment Methods

Personal Payment Methods are managed at the Person level. Personal Payment Method of a Person is associated with Organization Payment Method, Payment Type and his/her Bank Accounts which holds details like Account Type, Account Numbers, Bank, Bank Branch.

Manage Consolidation Groups

Navigator: Setup and Maintenance → Tasks → Search → Manage Consolidation Groups

Here we manage the Consolidation Groups which is associated with Legislative Data Group

Manage Salary Basis

Navigator: Setup and Maintenance → Tasks → Search → Manage Salary Basis

Here we manage the Salary Basis which holds the Pay Frequency, Element Mapping and Salary Ranges.

Manage Payroll Definitions

Navigator: Setup and Maintenance → Tasks → Search → Manage Payroll Definitions

Payroll definitions indicate the payment frequency and processing schedule. Payroll definitions associate workers with the payroll run through payroll relationships.

Manage Balance Definitions

Navigator: Setup and Maintenance → Tasks → Search → Manage Balance Definitions

Here we manage the Balances which have Balance Dimensions, Balance Feeds by Classification and Balance Feeds by Element.

Manage Element Classifications

Navigator: Setup and Maintenance → Tasks → Search → Manage Element Classifications

Here we manage Element Classifications like whether it's Earnings, Deductions, Information, etc... While Creating an Element, we select its Element Classification.

Manage Elements

Navigator: Setup and Maintenance → Tasks → Search → Manage Elements

We manage Elements as per the client's requirements. Some Elements are predefined. We need to add Input Values and create element eligibility records for the elements. We can also add Status Processing Rules and Balances to the Elements as per the requirement.

Manage Element Entries

Navigator: My Client Groups → Person Management (Enter Person Number) → Tasks → Manage Element Entries

We need to create all the required Element Entries to the Employees, which gets processed during Payroll Run.

Payroll Processes

A Basic Payroll Process is executed in Sequence below. There could be a few differences in Process as per the requirement.

- ☐ Calculate Payroll
- ☐ Calculate Prepayments
- ☐ Archive Periodic Payroll Results
- ☐ Make EFT Payments
- ☐ Generate Check Payments
- ☐ Generate Payslips

Roll Back Process is used to roll back the Required Payroll Run. Payroll Process can be executed manually in the above Sequence. But it would be better to create a Payroll Flow Pattern in the above sequence to automate the process.

Manage Payroll Flow Patterns

Navigator: Setup and Maintenance → Tasks → Search → Manage Payroll Flow Patterns

Payroll Flows are used to execute the Payroll Processes in required Sequence. So, we create a Payroll Flow Pattern as per the Requirement.

5.8 WEB SERVICES IN HCM

Introduction

A web service is a program that can be accessed remotely to achieve some required functionality. Web Services can be SOAP/ REST. SOAP uses XML for all messages, REST can use even smaller message formats that makes communication faster. In this chapter, we are going to see a Sample SOAP and REST Services that can be used in HCM.

SOAP in HCM

Navigator: Setup and Maintenance → Tools → Developer Connect

We need to use the Developer Connect portal to get the Web services details of the Business Objects. Below is a Sample WSDL File for Worker Service.

https://fs-your-cloud-hostname:443/hcmService/WorkerServiceV2?WSDL

Now, we are going to see a worked sample which involves the below steps to use Worker Service and CreateWorker Operation in Integration Cloud Service (ICS).

☐   **Create a SOAP Connection for the Worker Service as below :**

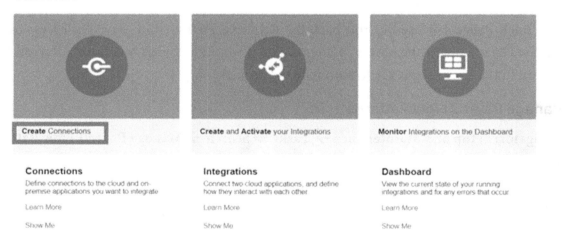

Click Create Connections and Select SOAP Adapter to create a New Connection (E.g., WorkerConnection)

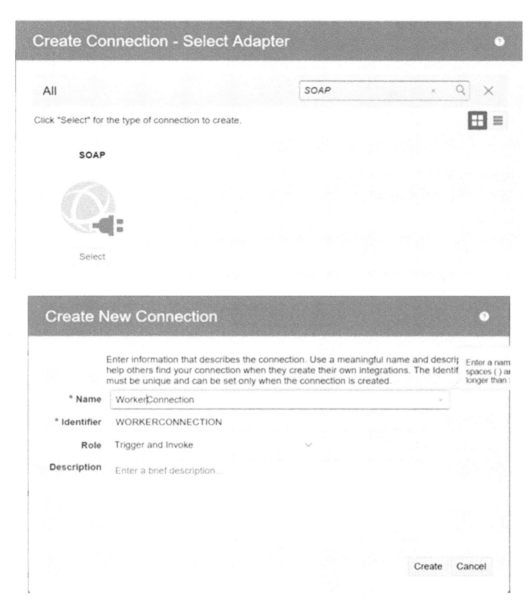

Then Click Configure Connectivity to specify the information to connect to your request.

Enter the WSDL URL

(https://fs-your-cloud-hostname:443/hcmService/WorkerServiceV2?WSDL) in the
Connection Properties Screen.

Then Click Configure Security to Specify the Login Credentials to access the Application.

Validate and Test the Connection.

☐ **Create Integration**

Start Here

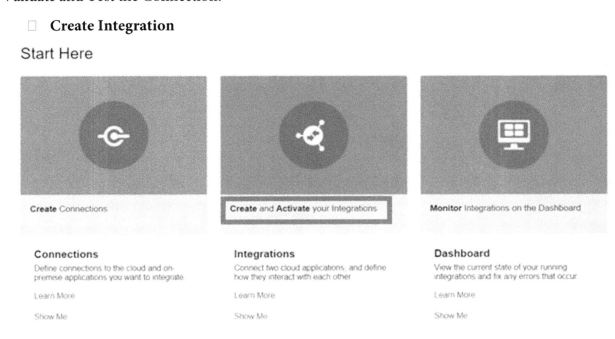

Connections
Define connections to the cloud and on-premise applications you want to integrate

Learn More

Show Me

Integrations
Connect two cloud applications, and define how they interact with each other

Learn More

Show Me

Dashboard
View the current state of your running integrations and fix any errors that occur

Learn More

Show Me

Click Create and Activate your integrations and Select Orchestration Style/Pattern to create a New Integration (E.g., CreateWorker)

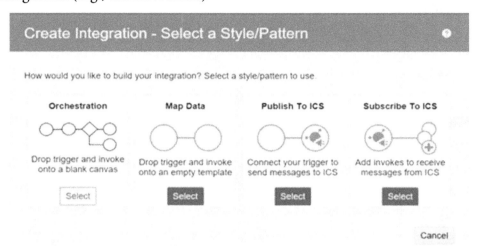

Invoke SOAP Connection created to the Orchestration and select CreateWorker operation to it, Save and Activate the integration.

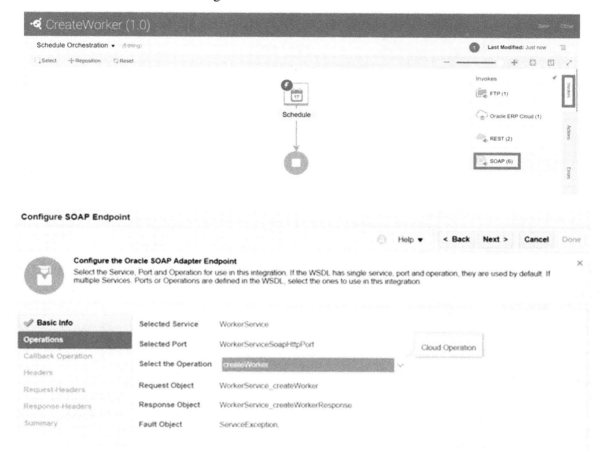

Finally, Map all the Mandatory Parameters as below :

Below Sample Payload which worked for reference. We can also automate it as per the requirement.

```
<soapenv:Header/>
<soapenv:Body>
<typ:createWorker>
<typ:AL>
<wor:RangeStartDate>2010-01-01</wor:RangeStartDate>
<wor:PersonNumber>620105</wor:PersonNumber>
<wor:StartDate>2010-01-01</wor:StartDate>
<wor:DateOfBirth>1984-08-08</wor:DateOfBirth>
<wor:ActionCode>ADD_PEN_WKR</wor:ActionCode>
<wor:WorkRelationship>
<wor:DateStart>2010-01-01</wor:DateStart>
<wor:PrimaryFlag>true</wor:PrimaryFlag>
<wor:LegalEmployerName>Wildfire Anthem</wor:LegalEmployerName>
<wor:WorkerType>P</wor:WorkerType>
<wor:ActionCode>ADD_PEN_WKR</wor:ActionCode>
<wor:WorkTerms>
<wor:ActionCode>ADD_PEN_WKR</wor:ActionCode>
<wor:AssignmentType>PT</wor:AssignmentType>
<wor:BusinessUnitShortCode>BUShortCode</wor:BusinessUnitShortCode>
<wor:EffectiveLatestChange>Y</wor:EffectiveLatestChange>
<wor:EffectiveSequence>1</wor:EffectiveSequence>
<wor:LegalEmployerName>LegalEmployerName</wor:LegalEmployerName>
<wor:PrimaryWorkTermsFlag>true</wor:PrimaryWorkTermsFlag>
```

118

```
<wor:RangeStartDate>2010-01-01</wor:RangeStartDate>
<wor:Assignment>
<wor:ActionCode>ADD_PEN_WKR</wor:ActionCode>
<wor:EffectiveSequence>1</wor:EffectiveSequence>
<wor:EffectiveLatestChange>Y</wor:EffectiveLatestChange>
<wor:AssignmentType>P</wor:AssignmentType>
<wor:AssignmentStatusTypeCode>ACTIVE_PROCESS</wor:AssignmentStatusTypeCod
e>
<wor:BusinessUnitShortCode>BUShortCode </wor:BusinessUnitShortCode>
<wor:AssignmentCategory>Full Time</wor:AssignmentCategory>
<wor:NormalHours>40</wor:NormalHours>
<wor:Frequency>Weekly</wor:Frequency>
<wor:LegalEmployerName>LegalEmployerName</wor:LegalEmployerName>
<wor:PrimaryAssignmentFlag>true</wor:PrimaryAssignmentFlag>
<wor:ProposedWorkerType>300000000214658</wor:ProposedWorkerType>
<wor:RangeStartDate>2010-01-01</wor:RangeStartDate>
<wor:AssignmentWorkMeasure>
<wor:Unit>FTE</wor:Unit>
<wor:Value>1</wor:Value>
<wor:RangeStartDate>2010-01-01</wor:RangeStartDate>
</wor:AssignmentWorkMeasure>
<wor:AssignmentWorkMeasure>
<wor:Unit>head</wor:Unit>
<wor:Value>1</wor:Value>
<wor:RangeStartDate>2010-01-01</wor:RangeStartDate>
</wor:AssignmentWorkMeasure>
</wor:Assignment>
</wor:WorkTerms>
</wor:WorkRelationship>
<wor:WorkerAddress>
<wor:RangeStartDate>2010-01-01</wor:RangeStartDate>
<wor:AddressType>HOME</wor:AddressType>
<wor:AddressLine1>143 Main Street</wor:AddressLine1>
<wor:AddressLine2>Line2</wor:AddressLine2>
<wor:TownOrCity>Henderson</wor:TownOrCity>
<wor:Region1>Clark</wor:Region1>
<wor:Region2>NV</wor:Region2>
<wor:Country>US</wor:Country>
<wor:PostalCode>89052</wor:PostalCode>
</wor:WorkerAddress>
<wor:WorkerEmail>
<wor:DateFrom>2010-01-01</wor:DateFrom>
<wor:EmailType>W1</wor:EmailType>
<wor:EmailAddress>Prathap.nagarajan@doyensys.com</wor:EmailAddress>
</wor:WorkerEmail>
```

```
<wor:WorkerLegislativeData>
<wor:RangeStartDate>2010-01-01</wor:RangeStartDate>
<wor:LegislationCode>US</wor:LegislationCode>
<wor:Sex>Male</wor:Sex>
</wor:WorkerLegislativeData>
<wor:WorkerName>
<wor:RangeStartDate>2010-01-01</wor:RangeStartDate>
<wor:LegislationCode>US</wor:LegislationCode>
<wor:NameType>GLOBAL</wor:NameType>
<wor:FirstName>Prathap</wor:FirstName>
<wor:LastName>Nagarajan</wor:LastName>
<wor:Title>MR.</wor:Title>
</wor:WorkerName>
</typ:AL>
<typ:pActionList>
<wor:ActionCode>ADD_PEN_WKR</wor:ActionCode>
</typ:pActionList>
</typ:createWorker>
</soapenv:Body>
</soapenv:Envelope>
```

REST in HCM

Now, let us discuss the steps to use REST Service to update the Manager of an Employee.

☐ **Create a REST Connection** (Follow the Steps same as above mentioned SOAP Connection)

☐ **Create Integration**
  o Click Create and activate your integrations and Select Orchestration Style/Pattern to create a New Integration for the REST Service.
  o **To get the Endpoint's relative resource URL for the REST Services, Please refer Oracle Documents.**
  o Invoke REST Connection created to the Orchestration and Configure REST endpoint as below, Save and activate the integration.
  o For Updating an Employee Assignment, Action EndPoint is **PATCH** and Endpoint's relative resource URL is

  **/hcmRestApi/resources/11.13.18.05/emps/{empsUniqID}/
  child/assignments/{assignmentsUniqID}**

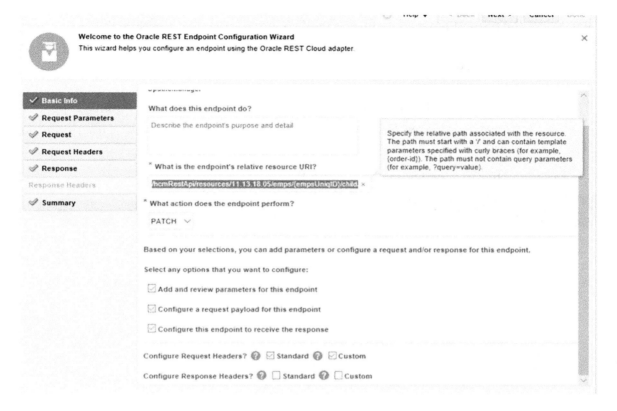

    o   Then, Select the Template Parameters as below:

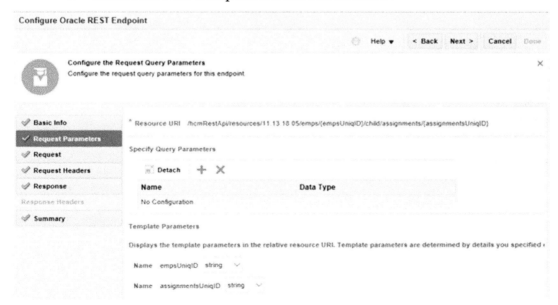

Then, Select the request payload format as JSON Sample and enter a sample JSON as

```
{ "ActionCode":"MANAGER_CHANGE", "ManagerId": 30000000XXXXXXX,
"ManagerAssignmentId": 30000000XXXXXXX, "ManagerType":
"LINE_MANAGER" }
```

- o Now, Select the Standard HTTP Header Name as Content-Type and Custom Header Name as Effective-Of and Custom Header Description as Range Date.
- o Finally, Map all the Mandatory Parameters as below:

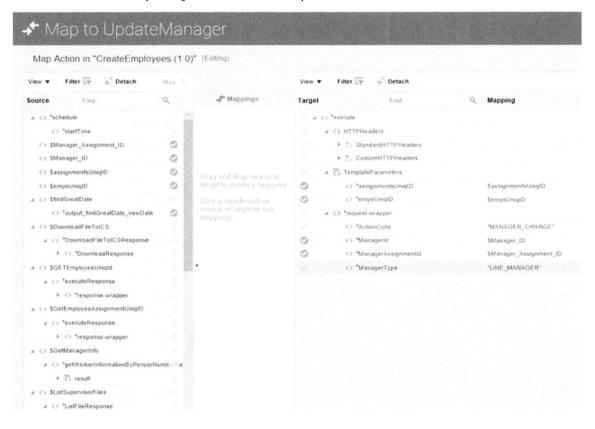

TECHNICAL IMPACT ANALYSIS FROM EBS TO CLOUD

6.1 INTRODUCTION TO TECHNICAL IMPACT ANALYSIS

Introduction

One of the pre-requisite for technical consideration when moving from Oracle E-Business Suite to Fusion Application is to understand the impact of database objects. This includes all the standards and customizations that are built-in in Oracle E-Business Suite. We should understand what are all can be re-built in Fusion Application and what cannot be done. To achieve this we need to have knowledge of what are all the database objects in Oracle E-Business Suite and what is the replacement for those in Fusion Applications.

Below are the major areas for which the technical impact analysis has to happen.

- Reports
- Integrations
- Customizations
- Extensions

Reports

The Reports developed in Oracle E-Business Suite using report builder and XML publisher can be re-developed in Fusion Applications using BI and OTBI reporting options. In order to re-develop this, we should have knowledge of Fusion database table replacements. Please refer "Table Similarities and Differences" topic for crucial table replacements experienced.

Integrations

In Oracle E-Business Suite most of the integrations are built using PL/SQL, SOAP & REST Web Service, XML Gateway platforms. Those integrations can be achieved in Fusion Applications using Oracle Integration Cloud Service (ICS), Process Cloud Service (PCS), Oracle Visual Builder Cloud Service (VBCS) and SOA Gateway.

Customizations

The customizations done in Oracle E-Business Suite are possible in Fusion Applications based on the product chosen. For example, all Reports & Approval Management can be customized in Fusion Application using BI and OTBI reporting options in all products SAAS, PAAS. Customizations in pages are not allowed in the SAAS model. But Form and OAF page customization in Oracle E-Business Suite can be achieved in the PAAS model using Java Could Service (JCS) and Database Cloud Service (DBCS).

Extensions

If any existing functionalities in the Oracle E-Business module do not meet the customer requirement then it can be achieved through an extension option. In Fusion Applications, the extensions can be achieved by leveraging the User Defined Tables UDT for storing custom details.

6.2 TABLE DIFFERENCES BETWEEN EBS AND FUSION

Introduction

To develop the Reports in Fusion Application BI Reports from Oracle E-Business Suite, it is mandatory to understand the table level impact. There are some cases like the same table structure is used with a different name, tables with the addition or deletion of columns, absolution of tables, one EBS table information is stored in two different tables and no change of tables between EBS and Fusion Application.

In this chapter, we have listed down the table similarities and differences in module wise which was experienced in real business cases of report developments.

Table Impact in Project Accounting Module

There is a significant table impact in the Project Accounting PA module. Some of the main tables experienced are listed below.

		EBS Table Name	Fusion Table Name
Project Accounting	Projects	PA_PROJECTS_ALL	PJF_PROJECTS_ALL_B PJF_PROJECTS_ALL_TL
		PA_PROJECT_TYPES_ALL	PJF_PROJECT_TYPES_B PJF_PROJECT_TYPES_TL
		PA_PROJECT_STATUSES	PJF_PROJECT_STATUSES_B PJF_PROJECT_STATUSES_TL
		PA_TASKS	PJF_PROJ_ELEMENTS_B PJF_PROJ_ELEMENTS_TL PJF_TASKS_V
		PA_TRANSACTION_SOURCES	PJF_TXN_SOURCES_B PJF_TXN_SOURCES_TL
		PA_COST_DISTRIBUTION_LINES_ALL	PJC_COST_DIST_LINES_ALL
		PA_IMPLEMENTATIONS_ALL	PJF_BU_IMPL_ALL
		PA_CUST_REV_DIST_LINES_ALL	PJB_REV_DISTRIBUTIONS
	Expenditures	PA_EXPENDITURE_TYPES	PJF_EXP_TYPES_B PJF_EXP_TYPES_TL PJF_EXP_TYPES_B_V
		PA_EXPENDITURE_ITEMS_ALL	PJC_EXP_ITEMS_ALL
		PA_EXPENDITURE_GROUPS	PJC_EXP_GROUPS_ALL
		PA_EXPENDITURE_COMMENTS	PJC_EXP_COMMENTS

Table Impact in HCM Module

Below are some of the table impacts in the Human Capital Management module.

		EBS Table Name	Fusion Table Name
Human Capital Management HCM	Person Details	PER_ALL_PEOPLE_F	PER_ALL_PEOPLE_F
			PER_PERSONS
			PER_PERSON_NAMES_F
			PER_PEOPLE_LEGISLATIVE_F
			PER_EMAIL_ADDRESSES
			PER_NATIONAL_IDENTIFIERS
	Assignments	PER_ALL_ASSIGNMENTS_F	PER_ALL_ASSIGNMENTS_M
		PER_JOBS	PER_JOBS_F
		PER_GRADES	PER_GRADES_F
		HR_ALL_POSITIONS_F	HR_ALL_POSITIONS_F
		HR_ALL_ORGANIZATION_UNITS	HR_ALL_ORGANIZATION_UNITS_F
		HR_LOCATIONS_ALL	HRW_LOCATIONS
	Absence	PER_ABSENCE_ATTENDANCES	ANC_PER_ABS_ENTRIES
		PER_ABS_ATTENDANCE_REASONS	ANC_ABSENCE_REASONS_F
		PER_ABSENCE_ATTENDANCE_TYPES	ANC_ABSENCE_TYPES_F
	Payroll	PAY_ALL_PAYROLLS_F	PAY_ALL_PAYROLLS_F
			PAY_REL_GROUPS_DN
			PAY_ASSIGNED_PAYROLLS_DN

PAY_PAYMENT_TYPES	PAY_PAYMENT_TYPES
PAY_ORG_PAYMENT_METHODS_F	PAY_ORG_PAY_METHODS_F
PAY_PERSONAL_PAYMENT_METHODS_F	PAY_PERSON_PAY_METHODS_F
PAY_PEOPLE_GROUPS	PAY_PEOPLE_GROUPS
PAY_ELEMENT_TYPES_F	PAY_ELEMENT_TYPES_F
PAY_INPUT_VALUES_F	PAY_INPUT_VALUES_F
PAY_ELEMENT_LINKS_F	PAY_ENTRY_USAGES
PAY_ELEMENT_ENTRY_VALUES_F	PAY_ELEMENT_ENTRY_VALUES_F
PAY_ELEMENT_ENTRIES_F	PAY_ELEMENT_ENTRIES_F
PAY_RUN_RESULTS	PAY_RUN_RESULTS
PAY_RUN_RESULT_VALUES	PAY_RUN_RESULT_VALUES
PAY_PAYROLL_ACTIONS	PAY_PAYROLL_ACTIONS
	PAY_PAYROLL_REL_ACTIONS
PAY_ASSIGNMENT_ACTIONS	PAY_PAYROLL_ASSIGNMENTS

Table Impact in Finance Module

Fusion Finance is extracted from Oracle E-Business Suite. So most of the tables in Finance modules like AP, AR, CM and GL are duplicated from EBS. Some of them may have only the name changes.

		EBS Table Name	Fusion Table Name
Finance	**AP**	AP_SUPPLIERS	POZ_SUPPLIERS
		AP_SUPPLIER_SITES_ALL	POZ_SUPPLIER_SITES_ALL_M
		AP_INVOICE_ALL	AP_INVOICE_ALL
		AP_INVOICE_LINES_ALL	AP_INVOICE_LINES_ALL
		AP_INVOICE_DISTRIBUTIONS_ALL	AP_INVOICE_DISTRIBUTIONS_ALL
	AR	HZ_CUST_ACCOUNTS	HZ_CUST_ACCOUNTS
		HZ_CUST_ACCT_SITES_ALL	HZ_CUST_ACCT_SITES_ALL
		HZ_CUST_SITE_USES_ALL	HZ_CUST_SITE_USES_ALL
		RA_CUSTOMER_TRX_ALL	RA_CUSTOMER_TRX_ALL
		RA_CUSTOMER_TRX_LINES_ALL	RA_CUSTOMER_TRX_LINES_ALL
	GL	GL_JE_HEADERS	GL_JE_HEADERS
		GL_JE_LINES	GL_JE_LINES
		GL_JE_BATCHES	GL_JE_BATCHES
		GL_JE_CATEGORIES	GL_JE_CATEGORIES
		GL_JE_SOURCES	GL_JE_SOURCES
		GL_SETS_OF_BOOKS	GL_SETS_OF_BOOKS
		GL_CODE_COMBINATIONS	GL_CODE_COMBINATIONS
	CM	CE_BANKS	CE_BANKS
		CE_BANK_BRANCHES	CE_BANK_BRANCHES
		CE_BANK_ACCOUNTS	CE_BANK_ACCOUNTS
		IBY_EXT_BANK_ACCOUNTS	IBY_EXT_BANK_ACCOUNTS

Table Impact in Fixed Assets Module

Fixed Assets module is extracted from Oracle E-Business Suite. So most of the tables in this module are duplicated from EBS.

		EBS Table Name	Fusion Table Name
Fixed Assets	FA	FA_DEPRN_PERIODS	FA_DEPRN_PERIODS
		FA_DEPRN_SUMMARY	FA_DEPRN_SUMMARY
		FA_ADDITIONS_B	FA_ADDITIONS_B
		FA_BOOKS	FA_BOOKS
		FA_CATEGORIES_B	FA_CATEGORIES_B
		FA_DEPRN_DETAIL	FA_DEPRN_DETAIL

DATA MIGRATION/CONVERSION

7.1 INTRODUCTION TO FUSION DATA MIGRATION

Introduction

Data migration is one of the main factors for implementing or upgrading any system. It is the process of transferring data between the source system and Fusion Applications.

Different ways to Migrate Data in Fusion Applications

- ☐ FBDI - File Based Data Import
- ☐ Spreadsheet Loader (ADFDI)
- ☐ HDL - HCM Data Loader
- ☐ Web Services

Best practices

- ☐ **Requirement Gathering:** Understand what data you are migrating, where it lives, what form it's in and the form it will take at its new destination.
- ☐ **Extract:** Extract the necessary data from the source system
- ☐ **Data Cleaning:** Perform data cleaning process to improve data quality, eliminate redundant or obsolete information, and match the requirements of the new system.
- ☐ **Data Mapping:** Map the necessary data and transform to the required structure. Apply transformation logic if any business-specific changes to be made.

- ☐ **Transform:** Implement data migration policies so data is moved in an orderly manner.
- ☐ **Reconciliation:** Test and validate in the target system the migrated data to ensure it is accurate.
- ☐ **Document:** Audit and document the entire data migration process

FBDI – File-Based Data Import

File-based data imports can be used to load data into Oracle Financials Cloud applications from external sources.

This is used when there is a need for high volume data uploads to Oracle ERP Cloud Service. It is used for both legacy data migration as well as the daily or regular import of data.

Use the file-based data import feature to import large volumes of data from third-party or other Oracle applications, or create new data in Oracle Fusion Cloud.

In a cloud environment, FBDI is the finest way to get mass conversions done in the shortest time. All entities are not provided with FBDI currently in Oracle Cloud.

Things to be considered before starting FBDI process

1. The machine should have Excel or equivalent software which can execute macros in Excel
2. For Excel, users should make sure the Macros are enabled
3. Check the FBDI template exists in the docs.oracle.com
4. It is better to download the FBDI template which has is of the same version as of the Cloud Environment.

Process Steps

1. Download the template from Cloud Environment
2. Prepare data in the template file
3. Generate the .zip files
4. Upload the file to oracle
5. Move data to Interface tables

6. Move data to Base tables

Spreadsheet Loader (ADFDI)

Spreadsheet loader can be used for small-to-medium levels of data volumes. The main pre-requisite is that the ADFDI plugin for MS Office should be installed in the user's machine.

It is ease and speed of use. Use of the standard Load Batch Data process provides error handling and is multithreaded.

Mass error correction can be done in spreadsheets and reprocess the error data.

Please refer "Payroll Batch Loader" under the "Fusion HCM" Chapter for the step-by-step process.

HDL - HCM Data Loader

HCM Data Loader is a well-built tool for bulk-loading and maintaining data. The data can be from any source. HCM Data Loader can be used for data migration, maintenance of HCM data where core HR data is uploaded regularly.

Business objects for most Oracle Fusion Human Capital Management (HCM) products can be loaded through HCM Data Loader. These products like Oracle Fusion Absence Management, Compensation, Global Human Resources, Global Payroll, Performance Management, Profile Management, Talent Review and Succession Management, and Workforce Management. Update of data also can be done on business objects using HCM Data Loader, regardless of how they were created.

It has an extensive user interface for data load, monitoring the progress and error review. It provides real-time information for all stages of its processing. HCM Data Loader's user interface includes detailed information about the component hierarchies and attributes of supported business objects.

Please refer "HCM Data Loader" under the "Fusion HCM" Chapter for the step by step process.

Web Services

Web Services are mainly used in Fusion Applications for Integrations. Data can be uploaded to Fusion Application using below two methods of Web Services.

☐ SOAP - Simple Object Access Protocol

☐ REST API's - Representational State Transfer Protocol

SOAP - Simple Object Access Protocol

A stateful protocol - It stores information about the payload and uses that information over a series of requests.

It uses HTTPS, JMS protocol for communication to and from the client and server.

It can only consume XML payloads.

It uses WSDL Web Service Description Language.

You can find the business objects in Fusion Application under Tools → Developer Connect

REST API's - Representational State Transfer Protocol

REST is a stateless protocol - the server does not store any state about the client session on the server-side.

It uses HTTPS requests and responses to process the data.

It can consume XML, JSON, plain text, HTML payloads.

It uses the WADL Web Application Description Language.

It's a lightweight protocol. SOAP has XML structure which requires starting as well as ending tags, thus increasing the network load as they have to travel over the network, which is not the case with REST.

7.2 DATA PREPARATION STRATEGY

Introduction

Data preparation is the most time-consuming and important part of the entire Fusion Data Migration process. It is the combined process of collecting, cleaning and consolidating the data from the different types of source systems.

Let us see how data can be prepared effectively in FBDI File Based Data Import.

Download FBDI Template

Download the appropriate template from the Oracle website. Oracle has given the repository to download all the FBDI templates. The best practice is to get the latest template downloaded for the version of Fusion Application in which data migration is supposed to happen.

Follow the below navigation to download from the Oracle website.

Navigation: docs.oracle.com → Cloud → Applications → Procurement (select your version here from the drop-down) → Books → File-Based Data Import for Oracle Procurement Cloud → Expand and Select Item → Download the template

Development

File-Based Data Import for Oracle Procurement Cloud

HTML

Describes file-based data imports to import or update legacy and other data into Oracle Procurement Cloud from external applications.

In the screenshot below, the Supplier Model is given for example.

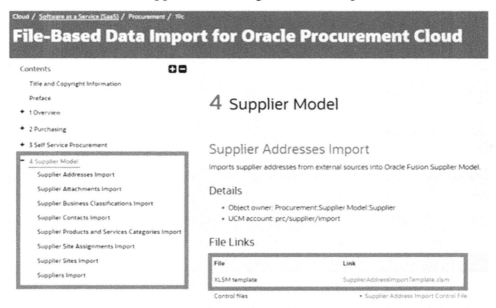

In every FBDI templates, the basic information is given in the first worksheet as shown below.

For example, the simple instructions to prepare and load the data, interface tables in which data is going get populated and Control Files being used for loaders.

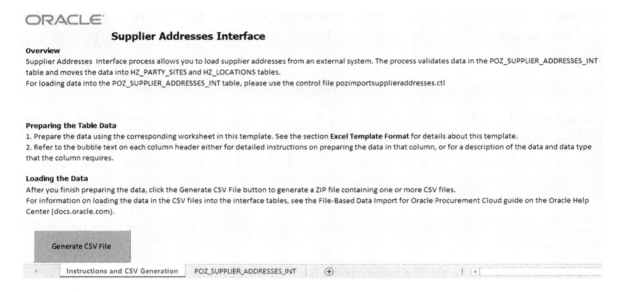

Prepare Data

The next worksheet is the real sheet where the actual data which is going to load should present.

The above example has only one sheet for data. In some of the templates like Supplier Bank Accounts, Payable Invoices & Receivable Invoices will have more than one datasheet.

The POZ_SUPPLIER_ADDRESSES_INT datasheet has the list of fields from business objects which can be uploaded to Fusion Applications. In which there are some key fields are mandatory and some are optional. The mandatory fields can be found by the '*' symbol on the end of each field as shown below.

Supplier Addresses Interface	Show Additional Attributes					
* Required						
Batch ID	Import Action *	Supplier Name*	Address Name *	Country	Address Line 1	City
Batch_A12345	UPDATE	Advance Networ	MAIN-PURCH			
Batch_A12345	CREATE	Advance Networ	MAIN-PAY	USA	90 Edgewater Drive	Belmont

Batch ID – It is an optional identifier. Better to provide a constant value so that while scheduling an import process it would be easy to identify records from the interface table for monitoring.

Import Action – Only CREATE and UPDATE actions are possible through the FBDI process.

Generate .zip File

Along with Batch ID and Import Action, populate all the necessary information along with mandatory fields. Once the data is ready, click on the "Generate CSV File" button from the first worksheet of the template to generate the .zip file which contains actual .csv file to upload to Fusion Application.

7.3 DATA VALIDATION TECHNIQUES

Introduction

Before attempting standard import programs it is very essential to validate and rectify the data for the smooth import process. Unlike the Oracle E-Business Suite, Fusion Applications does not allow us to create custom Database objects to place the data and validate it against the instance. So it has become a tedious job for technical consultants to compare the lookup values exist in the data and configuration setups against Fusion Application. The validation process includes checking whether an object already exists on the target system and whether the user is authorized to create or modify the object.

Best Practice Followed

One of the effective ways to validate and also to apply transformation logic on the data is the use of existing Oracle E-business Suite Database. The whole process is explained in the process steps below.

- Create Custom Tables
- Load Data into Staging Table
- Create Fusion Reports for lookups
- Perform Validation and Transformation Logics and load into Template Table

☐ Extract data from Template Table

Custom Tables

Like the conversion process in Oracle E-Business Suite, create the below tables in the database.

Staging Tables: This is for holding the raw data from the source system. Create the table with column sequence the same as the raw data field sequence.

Template Tables: This is for holding data in Fusion FBDI format. Create the table with column sequence the same as the sequence of the FBDI fields so that it is easy to take the extract and apply in the FBDI template.

Template Tables: This is for holding setup values and lookup values from Fusion Application.

Load Data into Staging Table

The raw data can be loaded to the staging table using the methods below based on the complexity.

☐ SQL*Loader
☐ TOAD Data import option
☐ External tables

The best option is to load using External Tables because, in future data migration for different customers, the same script can be used just by altering the External table fields to fit the raw data fields.

Fusion Reports for lookups

In order to validate the setup values and lookup values in raw files, it is necessary to bring those values from Fusion Application to the Database where the pre-validation is going to happen. This can be achieved by creating Lookup Report in Fusion Application, extract the report data and load it into custom lookup tables.

For example, if the Supplier Bank Accounts are getting migrated then values like Supplier Number, Bank, Branch and Country Lookups have to be pulled from Fusion Application to validate against raw data.

There are three ways to extract data from Fusion applications.

☐ BI Publisher Report
☐ OTBI Analysis
☐ HCM Extracts

In the above three, the quick option is OTBI analysis. It's a predefined data model provided by Oracle itself. If the required fields are available in the OTBI subject area then report can be created by just drag and drop option.

If required fields are not available in the OTBI subject area, the BI Publisher report can be created by leveraging underlying standard table objects. The complex logics can be built using the BI utilities like report triggers and the use of PL/SQL codes using WITH clause.

Please refer to "Reporting in Cloud" chapter for how to create reports.

Once the reports are created with required values, download the output in the desired format like Excel or Text to get the data loaded into Lookup tables using SQL*Loader or TOAD Import Data option.

Perform Validation and Transformation Logics

Now the raw data and lookup values are available in the same database tables. The validation should be done for each lookup values and if any missing values then it should be reported through error tables, so that once validation is completed, the error table report can give the list of missing values to get defined in Fusion Application. To re-validate the data, the new extract report has to be taken from Fusion Application and reloaded to lookup tables.

7.4 IMPORT & RECONCILIATION

Introduction

Navigator

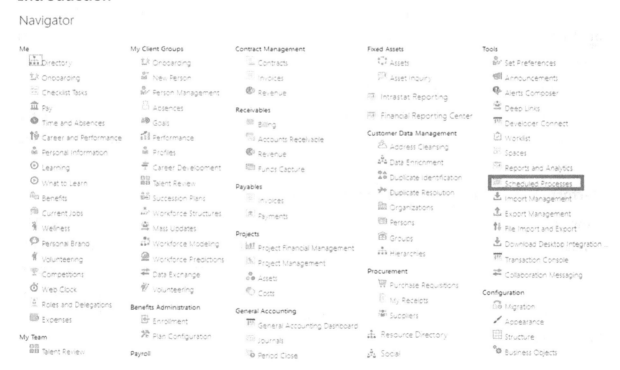

The Import & Reconciliation processes are more similar as in Oracle E-Business Suite. The "Scheduled Process" window is the new look of the Submit Request Form of Oracle E-

Business Suite. For reconciliation, the imported data can be extracted through the BI or OTBI report.

Login into Fusion Applications, click on the Taskbar on the left top corner and go for "Scheduled Process" to run the standard import programs.

Upload .zip File

Click on the "Schedule New Process" button and Select the process "Load Interface File for Import" and click on OK.

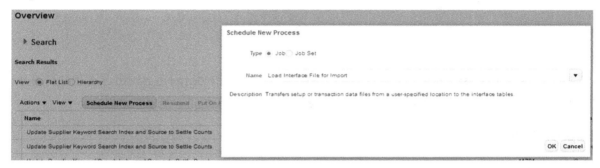

On the next screen, there are two input parameters such as "Import Process" & "Data File".

Import Process: Select the standard import process (For Example "Import Supplier Addresses" in this case). This will decide that the actual data from in .zip file should get inserted into which interface tables (in this case it should be POZ_SUP_ADDRESSES_INT).

Data File: Choose the .zip generated using FBDI template from system Using "Upload a New File" option from the drop-down and click on Submit.

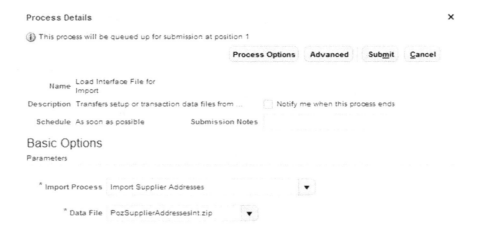

This process will insert the data from PozSupplierAddressInt.zip into POZ_SUP_ADDRESSES_INT interface table.

Import Process

To submit a standard import process again go for "Schedule New Process" and select "Import Supplier Addresses". Then select the parameters as per the need.

Import Option: New – processes only records with status "New". Rejected – Processes only records with status "Rejected". All – processes both New & Rejected.

Report Exceptions Only: Decides whether the output file should include only exception or the overall summary of the process.

Batch Id: This will decide which records from the interface table should get processed. The Batch Id value from the FBDI template should be given here. If no value is provided, only records without a Batch Id will be processed.

Once the program completes, the report summary output along with error details and the log details will be available in Attachments.

Reconciliation

It's a process of verification where the target or migrated data is compared with original source data to ensure that the migration activity has transferred the data correctly. It is expected that there are mistakes in the mapping and transformation logic. These problems can lead to different issues such as

- Missing records
- Missing values
- Incorrect values
- Duplicated records
- Badly formatted values
- Broken relationships across tables or systems

These issues cannot be identified without the data reconciliation process and will destruct the overall accuracy of data. This can be done by taking the loaded data extract from Fusion Application using BI or OTBI reports and compare using the Excel Lookup option.

The typical approach for data reconciliation mostly depends on simple record counts to observe whether the expected number of records had been migrated. This way we can ensure that no records are missed.

To address the other issues, excel VLOOKUP option or other third-party tools can be used.

7.5 COMMON ISSUES FACED

Introduction

This section covers the list of issues faced during the implementation phase along with if any solution achieved and the tips and tricks for a smooth Fusion Data Conversion strategy.

- ☐ Date Formats – Make sure that all the date fields are formatted in "YYYY/MM/DD" for FBDI and HCM Data Loader and "YYYY-MM-DD" for Payroll Batch Loader. If not then the loader program "Load Interface File for Import" will get "error" out for an invalid date.

- ☐ Always it is better to generate the .zip file through the FBDI template. There are some options where we can generate files using UTL_FILE utility on the server and can zip in the local system. Sometimes faced issues in upload file due to junk characters getting appended in file generation or transfer process.

- ☐ In FBDI and HCM Data Loader, the .csv and .dat files should be in the same naming convention as per Oracle standard given in docs.oracle.com. If not then the loader program may end up in error. But the .zip file names can be changed as per the wish.

- ☐ Like Oracle E-Business Suite, the supplier sites are visible to only the users who have the Buyer setup enabled. Otherwise only supplier account and contact information can be seen.

- ☐ While migrating bank branches through Rapid Implementation, you can face an issue "Branch Number cannot be more than # characters". "#" → Varied based on the country for which the bank was created. This was rectified by disabling country-specific bank validations in Cash Management Profile options. Please refer the screenshot below.

- ☐ **Navigation:** Setup & Maintenance → Global Search → Type "Cash Management Profile Options" → Search with "Disable Country Specific Bank Validations"

Manage Cash Management Profile Options

◢ Search : Profile Option

Profile Option Code		Application		∨
Profile Display Name	Disable Country Specific Bank Valic	Module	▾	
Category		∨		

Search Results

◢ Search Results : Profile Options

Actions ▾ View ▾ Detach

Profile Option Code	Profile Display Name	Application	Module	Description
CE_DISABLE_BANK_VAL	Disable Country Specific Bank Validations	Cash Management	Shared Setup	Disable country specific bank validations.

Columns Hidden 2

◢ CE_DISABLE_BANK_VAL : Profile Values

Actions ▾ View ▾ ✚ ✖ ⬚ Detach

* Profile Level	Product Name	User Name	▲ ▾	Profile Value
Site				No

- ☐ There might be some field values with leading zeros. When copying it from the database table to FBDI templates, it may disappear if the template cell format is "General". This can be resolved by changing the template cell format to "Text". So the best practice is to change all the cell formats to "Text" before attempting to copy data.

- ☐ Check the execution reports once the import program is complete. For some programs, even if the status is 'Succeeded', there might be some errors reported in the output. So the execution report should be reviewed to avoid any discrepancies.

- ☐ In some templates, there might be more than one sheet. One sheet may have reference values or foreign key relations to others. So a cross-validation should also be done to avoid any wrong parent and child links.

- ☐ Oracle has given specific comments for each column in templates. Even there are some comments which are very specific on how configured should be in Fusion

Application, field formats like date format and list of lookups that are accepted for the import process. It's better to read the comments before data preparation.

☐ Make sure that a value is provided for all the mandatory fields in the template. This can be identified by trailing '*' character in each field.

☐ In GL Import faced an issue "Cross-Validation Rules: The segment value is invalid for this company". There is a validation configuration for code combination values generation. This error might occur if the given segment value is not covered in the validation range. Oracle has given provision to bypass the specific values in this validation.

To resolve this issue add those segment values in the "Validation Filter" field with a corresponding expression like "Company segment – is not equal to '000'".

☐ **Navigation:** Setup & Maintenance → Manage Cross Validation Rules → Search for the segment like "IC" → Enter the segment values in "Validation Filter" field.

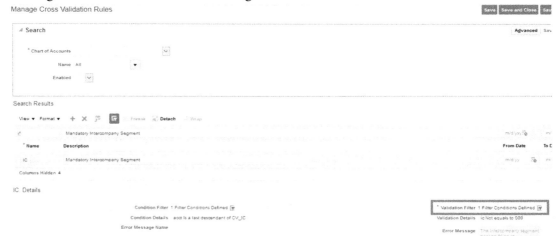

☐ All the import error details can be viewed in interface error tables for each import. Some of the main Interface Error tables are

POZ_SUPPLIER_INT_REJECTIONS: This table will hold all the supplier element import error details.

RA_INTERFACE_ERRORS_ALL: This table stores information about interface data that failed the AutoInvoice validation step.

AP_INTERFACE_REJECTIONS: This table stores information about invoice data from the AP_INVOICES_INTERFACE and AP_INVOICE_LINES_INTERFACE tables which could not be processed by Payables Open Interface Import.

HRC_DL_MESSAGE_LINES: This table is used for logging ERRORS/WARNINGS occurred during TRANSFER, IMPORT, LOAD and VALIDATE processes.

HRC_DL_LOGICAL_LINES: This table contains Logical Rows for the data provided in the DAT file. Each Logical Row corresponds to one or more physical lines in HRC_DL_PHYSICAL_LINES. It also holds information on its status value during IMPORT, LOAD and VALIDATE which helps to calculate status counts for a given data set business Object.

INTEGRATIONS TO CLOUD - WEB SERVICES

8.1 REMOTE CONNECTIVITY MADE EASY – APP-TO-APP INTERFACE IN ORACLE EBS

With the growing demands of data in the enterprises, there are multiple applications being used for various purposes to achieve end-user requirements. When there are several applications being used, there arises the need for connecting all of them irrespective of their platform, language or server location, etc.

Web Services can be SOAP/ REST. SOAP uses XML for all messages, REST can use even smaller message formats that makes communication faster. In this chapter, let us discuss the REST Webservice that is recommended by Oracle for providing interoperability between remote systems/ applications.

REST is Representational State Transfer. It is an architectural style that specifies a uniform interface to enable services to connect different systems over the Web. It is a client/ server architecture and is designed to use the HTTP Protocol. Data and Functionality are considered as resources. So the client and servers exchange these resources using the Uniform Resource Identifiers (URI).

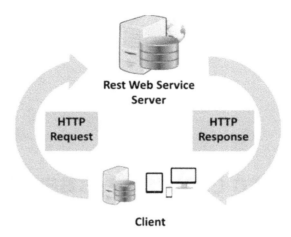

A Web Service that uses REST is called REST or RESTful Web Services. It is a collection of open protocols and standards for exchanging data. RESTful services are fast, simple and lightweight. It supports XML and JSON formats which is smaller in size. It is described in WADL (Web Application Description Language) and no expensive tools are required to interact with the Web Service. It can be learned quickly by developers and no extensive processing is required. Having said all this, the implementation of the REST service is definitely simpler as compared to SOAP. But REST is not a standard and its implementation varies to suit different application needs

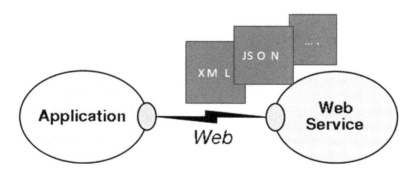

8.2 INTRODUCTION TO WEB SERVICES IN EBS

Most businesses using Oracle EBS have other applications that have to interact with the ERP system. Data transfer to and from the EBS system is required for efficient interfacing of data and also to have the different applications in sync with each other.

To enable the EBS system to effectively communicate with each other, Oracle has provided the ISG (Integrated SOA Gateway) from 12.1 version for consuming SOAP-based Web Services. From EBS 12.2.3, ISG has been enhanced as an infrastructure to provide and consume REST-based services.

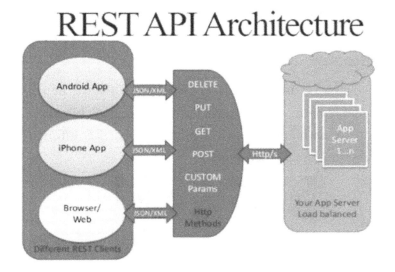

REST API uses the HTTP protocol that has the following operations/ methods:

- DELETE – deletes a resource
- PUT – creates a new resource
- GET – retrieves the current state of the resource
- POST – transfers a new data onto a resource

EBS uses PL/SQL API for POST operations and JAVA API for GET operations. Applications and their features exchange data and information through defined APIs. EBS business functionality/ data can be exposed to the remote system irrespective of the platform or the language of the originating application. This helps to query data as well as write data to and from the remote data sources.

The REST API breaks down a transaction to create a series of small modules. Each module addresses a particular underlying part of the transaction.

REST Web Service provides a common data access layer that can be accessed from any platform and can be called from your Web browser. It is highly scalable, supports caching and is lightweight.

Being stateless it reduces the overhead and complexity of the server. These web services are recommended by Oracle to develop custom mobile apps for Oracle EBS applications.

ISG in EBS – Integration Repository

ISG (Integrated SOA Gateway) is the gateway in Oracle EBS for deploying REST Web Services and service enablement. Oracle seeded APIs are available to be used from the Integration Repository. Custom interfaces can also be used if the functionality required cannot be achieved using the Oracle seeded API.

Oracle Integrated SOA (Service Oriented Architecture) is a complete set of service infrastructure to provide and administer Oracle EBS Web Services. It is a centralized repository that contains numerous interface endpoints within EBS. ISG supports the functionality to expose these integration interfaces published in the integration Repository as SOAP and REST-based web services.

It supports PL/SQL APIs, JAVA APIs, concurrent programs, XML gateway, Business events, etc. to be exposed as Web Services.

Configuring REST Services in ISG

The steps involved in configuring REST services in Integrated SOA Gateway in Oracle EBS are given in the flowchart below.

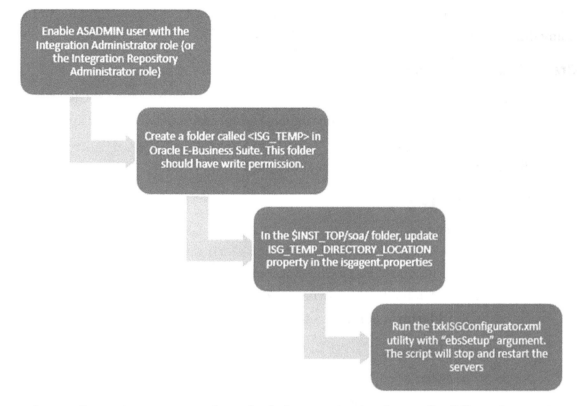

Once the configurations are complete, the below navigation has to be followed to activate REST Web Services.

- Manage REST service lifecycle activities
- Search and deploy the desired APIs as REST services
- View deployed services through WADL descriptions
- Grant user access privileges for the services
- Testing and Validating the REST Services

8.3 IMPLEMENTING WEB SERVICES IN CLOUD USING ICS

Introduction

Integration Cloud Service (ICS) is a PaaS cloud offering from Oracle that provides capabilities of integrating applications both on-cloud and on-premise. ICS provides a rich set of connectors/adapters to connect to Oracle's SaaS and on-premise applications and many third-party cloud and on-premise applications.

Oracle Integration Features

- ☐ Connects your applications, on-premise with Cloud (Integration Cloud Service) and helps in design, monitor, and manage connections between your applications
- ☐ Automate & Manage business Process (Process Cloud Service)
- ☐ Build Applications Visually (Visual Builder Cloud Service)

Steps to Follow for ICS

- ☐ Create an Instance.

    Provide all the details to create an instance as mentioned below:

    - o Sign in to your Oracle Cloud account.
    - o Click ▤ in the top left corner of the Oracle Cloud Infrastructure Console.
    - o Click **Platform Services** > **Integration**.

1. Click **Create Instance**.

    - o The Instance page is displayed.
    - o Specify the following details:

Field	Description
Instance Name	Enter an instance name that is unique within the tenant domain. The name cannot have more than 30 characters, must start with a letter, and can contain only letters and numbers.
Description	Enter a description to identify this new service. The description is used only in the instance list display.
Notification Email	Enter an email address at which to be notified of instance provisioning progress (for example, when provisioning completes).

Field	Description
Region	Select the compute region from which to perform the installation. Otherwise, select **No Preference**.
Tags	Select available tags for assignment or click the icon to define new tags and assign to the service instance. You can use tags to search for and categorize your instances.
Identity Domain	Select the identity domain to identify users and resources associated with the provisioned service instance.
License Type	Select an option: ☐ Select to bring an existing Oracle Fusion Middleware license to the cloud for use with Oracle Integration. ☐ Select to create a new Oracle Integration license.

- o When complete, click **Next**.
- o And Provide the following details

Field	Description
Number of 5k Messages Per Hour Packs	Enter a value between 1 and 12. A single pack enables you to send up to 5000 messages per hour. This option is displayed if you selected to subscribe to a new Oracle Integration software license.
Number of 20k	Enter a value between 1 and 3. A single pack enables you to send

Field	Description
Messages Per Hour Packs	up to 20,000 messages per hour. This option is displayed if you selected to bring an existing Oracle Middleware software license to Oracle Integration.
Feature Set	Displays the available feature sets. Visual Builder is automatically installed with each set. ☐ **Integration**: Installs the Integrations feature set. ☐ **Integration and Process**: Installs the Integrations and Processes feature sets.

o When complete, click **Next**.

o Confirm your selections; then click **Confirm**.

o Wait for the installation to complete.

Once Instance is Created you can see the screenshot given below.

Overview

Instance Overview   As of Sep 29, 2019 7:54:08 AM UTC

Status: Creating service ..   Version: 19.3.3.190924.1600-31520
Active: Yes   Feature Set: Integration and Process
Message Packs: 0   Oracle Integration Edition: Enterprise Edition
Service Identifier: 602326960   IDCS Application: OICINST_Suryatest1234
License: Cloud License

In-Progress Operation Messages

Create Service In Progress   Start Time: Sep 29, 2019 7:50:49 AM UTC
Instance Name: Suryatest1234
Operation: Create Service
Operation Status: Running

☐ Once you have created an Instance of Oracle Integration, navigate the Oracle Integration home page and click on **Integrations** and it will show all the options available there.

- o **Integrations**: Integrations are processes that utilize connections (among other things) to implement a business process.

- o **Connections**: Connections are the various connectors that can be utilized to communicate with external applications. Communication can be done with conventional systems like File, FTP, etc., and also with new social media and other applications, like LinkedIn, Facebook, Twitter, Evernote, etc.

- o **Lookups**: A bit like DVMs in SOA Suite, can cross-reference values of the same attribute/element when mapping from one system to another.

- o **Packages**: A bit like partitions in EM console, can be used to group together similar integrations.

- o **Agents**: Agents are used to connecting to on-premise applications. For example, if you are using on-premise systems like ERP/SAP and also using Oracle OIC in the same implementation, you would have to use an agent to connect to the OIC application.

- o **Adapters**: Adapters lists all the adapters that are available for external communication. Currently, about 50 adapters are offered.

Steps to create a sample Integration

Step1: Create Adapter Connection

Connections define information about the instances of each configuration you are integrating.

☐ Sign in to your Oracle Integration Cloud instance: http://*host:port*/ic.

☐ Click the **Got it!** button to dismiss any text overlays that are displayed.

☐ On the Home page, click **Create Connections**.

☐ In the upper right corner, click **Create**.

☐ Enter REST in the **Search** field, then click the **Search** icon

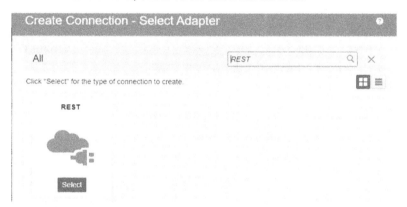

☐ Select **REST**. The Create New Connection dialog is displayed.

☐ In the **Name** field, enter Hello World.

☐ From the **Role** list, select **Trigger**

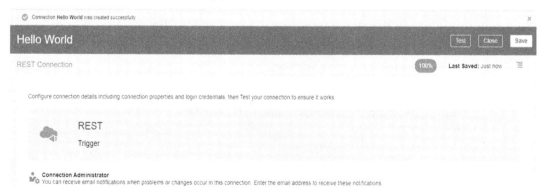

☐ In the **Email** field, enter an email address to receive email notifications when problems or changes occur in this connection. Note that a security policy of **Basic Authentication** is automatically selected. No additional configuration is required.

☐ In the upper right corner, click **Test**. The message Connection **Hello World** was tested successfully is displayed.

☐ Click **Save**, then click **Close**.

Step2: Create Integration

Integrations are the main ingredient of Oracle Integration Cloud. When you create your integration, you build on the connections you already created by defining how to process the data for the connections.

☐ In the navigation pane on the left, click **Integrations**.

☐ In the upper right corner, click **Create**.

☐ Select **App Driven Orchestration** as the pattern to use. The Create New Integration dialog is displayed.

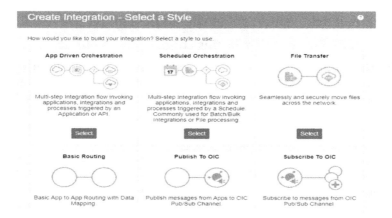

☐ In the **What do you want to call your integration?** Field, enter MyFirstIntegration, and then click **Create.**

The integration canvas is displayed. You are now ready to design your first integration.

Step3: Design your Integration:

☐ In the right navigation pane, click **Triggers**.

☐ Click **REST**, then drag the **Hello World** connection to the + sign

Description of the illustration rest_adapter_drag.

The Adapter Endpoint Configuration wizard is displayed.

☐ On the Basic Info page, enter the following details, then click **Next**:

Field	Description
What do you want to call your endpoint?	helloWorld
What is the endpoint's relative resource URI?	/{message}
What action does the endpoint perform?	**GET**
Select any options that you want to configure	Select the following: **Add and review parameters for this endpoint** **Configure this endpoint to receive the response**

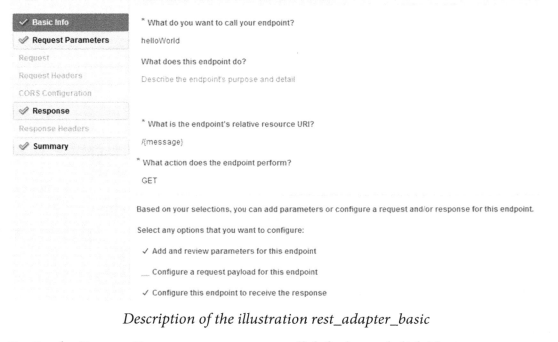

Description of the illustration rest_adapter_basic

☐ On the Request Parameters page, accept all defaults, and click **Next**.

☐ On the Response page, select **JSON Sample** in the **Select the response payload file** section.

Click **<<<inline>>>,** and enter the following message in the JSON sample field.

{ "Message":"message", "Welcome":"Welcome to ICS! You have now designed your first integration!"}

☐ Click **Ok.**

☐ In the **Select the type of payload with which you want the endpoint to reply** section, select **JSON**; then click **Next**.

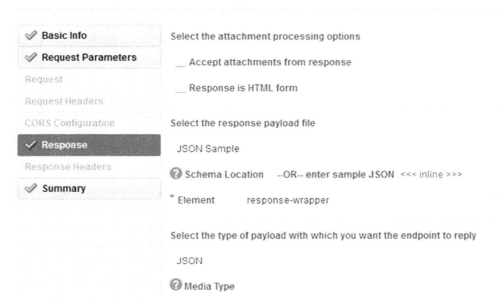

Description of the illustration rest_adapter_response

On the Summary page, review your selections, then click **Done**

Description of the illustration summary

- [ ] In the right navigation pane, click **Actions**.
- [ ] Drag a **Logger** action immediately below **helloWorld**. A + sign is displayed.
- [ ] Place the **Logger** action inside the + sign. The Create Action dialog is displayed.
- [ ] In the **Name** field, enter logMessage, then click **Create**.
- [ ] In the **Log** section, click **Always**.

In the **Logger Message** section, click the **Edit** icon.

* **Logger Message**   Specify what message should display in the Activity Stream. You specify the message by adding an expression. You can define a static message or include variables to be logged with the message.

Description of the illustration logger_expression

☐ Select the **message** element in the **Source** tree and click the > sign. The syntax /nssrcmpr:execute/nssrcmpr:TemplateParameters/nsmpr*number*:message is displayed in the **Expression** field.

☐ Click the **Refresh** icon to the right of **Expression Summary**. The message element is displayed.

Click **Validate** to show a message at the top indicating that the expression is valid, then click **Close**.

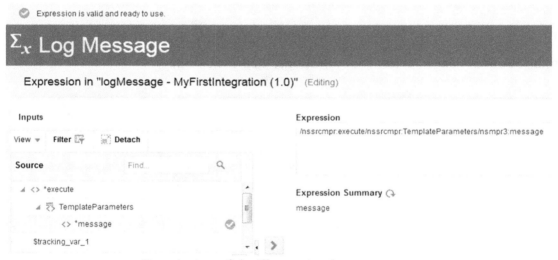

Description of the illustration logger_syntax

Click **Close** to return to the integration canvas. *Description of the illustration integration_partial*

helloWorld

logMessage

Map to helloWorld

☐ Click the **Map to helloWorld** icon, and then click the **Edit** icon. The mapper is displayed. The mapper enables you to map the source data structure to the target data structure.

In the **Source** section, drag the **message** element to the **Message** target element. A green line connecting the two elements is displayed.

Description of the illustration mapper_mapping

☐ In the **Target** section, click the **Welcome** element. The Build Mappings page is displayed.

☐ Replace -- Drag and Drop or Type value here... with the following text: "Welcome to ICS!!! Echo was successful."

Click **Save**, then click **Close** to return to the mapper

Description of the illustration mapper

☐ Click **Validate**. The following message is displayed: Mapping is valid and ready to use.

☐ Click **Close**, then click **Apply** if prompted to apply your changes before exiting.

From the **Actions** menu in the upper right, select **Tracking**. Business identifiers enable runtime tracking of messages.*Description of the illustration tracking_action*

In the **Source** section, drag the **message** element to the first row of the **Tracking Field** column, then click **Save**.

Description of the illustration business_id

☐ View the completed integration.

    ○ A REST Adapter is configured as a trigger (inbound) connection to invoke the integration.

    ○ A logging message is created and logged to the activity stream. A browser response is sent to you.

    ○ A mapper is configured to map the source and target data structures.

Description of the illustration designed_integration

☐ Click **Save**, then click **Close**. The Design is now complete.

Step4: Activate and Running the Integration:

In the row for the **MyFirstIntegration** integration, click the **Activate** icon, and then click **Activate** when prompted.

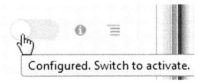

Description of the illustration activate_button

☐ Wait for the icon to turn green, indicating that the integration is activated. The following message is displayed in the green banner at the top of the page: Integration **MyFirstIntegration (1.0)** was activated successfully.

☐ Click the icon immediately to the right of the **Activate** icon to display a popup message.

☐ Click the endpoint URL in the message to access the Endpoint Description page.

```
https://hostname:port/ic/api/integration/v1/flows/rest/MYFIRS
TINTEGRATION/1.0/metadata
```

☐ View the following response in your browser:

```
{
   "Message" : "Invoking my first integration.",
   "Welcome" : "\"Welcome to ICS!!!  Echo was successful.\""
}
```

This Completes our Sample Integration Process.

For more on Integrations Cloud Please go through the below link:

https://docs.oracle.com/en/cloud/paas/integration-cloud/index.html

MOBILE APPS IN FUSION APPLICATIONS

9.1 INTRODUCTION TO ORACLE CLOUD MOBILE APP

Mobile is everywhere and has changed the facet of our lives. More than 50% of the world's population now carries a smartphone. Expectations of how we as consumers engage through mobile have influenced how customers the business partners expect to engage with you. Mobile apps that delight and engage end-users are now a fundamental component of any successful organization's digital strategy.

You might already know that the Oracle EBS provides many mobile apps to do our transaction, approvals and other key activities. The same way Fusion cloud also enables us to access the cloud features on the mobile device. It can be installed on the Oracle HCM Cloud app on Android and iOS-based smartphones and tablets.

The Cloud mobile app supports mobile responsive pages on the phone. On a tablet, we can access both classic as well as mobile responsive features. The mobile app authenticates based on the role and doesn't require any additional mobile-specific configuration.

Oracle Procurement Cloud Mobile App

The Oracle Procurement Cloud Self Service Procurement Mobile application allows us to take self-service shopping and requisition creation on the road. Employees in the field or on the go can easily and quickly create and submit requisitions from iOS and Android devices. The mobile application is easy to use, with a consumer experience that includes the ability to view item details in search results, view the status of recent requisitions, and keep up-to-date with purchasing news.

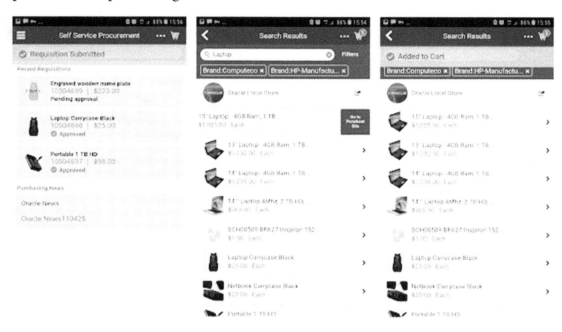

HCM Cloud Mobile app

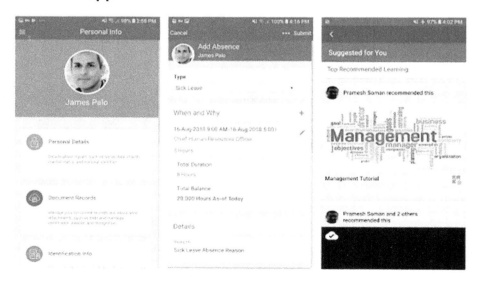

HCM Cloud Mobile app gives organizations secure access to their Oracle HCM Cloud Application while on the go. The same responsive user experience enabled in the web application is available in this mobile app, and provides a seamless and consistent experience when managing yourself, your team, and your organization.

Below are some of the features we available in HCM cloud mobile apps

- ☐ View and manage your onboarding tasks before the first day of work.
- ☐ Manage personal information, view payslip, manage goals, view and manage benefits elections, manage skills and qualifications, look up colleagues in the directory, and much more.
- ☐ Hire an employee, promote, transfer, change the working hours, and manage salary and compensation of current employees.
- ☐ Use My Team to stay informed of team's overall employment, compensation, and talent information.
- ☐ Users can also view their notifications and approve or reject a request from their mobile device using this application

Installing and Configuring Oracle mobile apps

We can install mobile applications on mobile devices with Android and iOS operating systems (OS).

To install and connect to Oracle HCM Cloud:

- ☐ Download respective Oracle cloud Mobile from the app store or play store. On Android devices, you have to download and manually install the mobile app.
- ☐ Accept the end-user license agreement (EULA) to proceed to the sign-in page. From there on, you will have the same user experience on the desktop and mobile.
- ☐ On the Getting Started page, enter your Cloud application URL. For example:
  - o Cloud Desktop URL: https://xyz111-fa.us.oracle.com
  - o Cloud Mobile URL: xyz111-fa.us.oracle.com
  - o This is the same URL you enter in your mobile or desktop browser. If you can't access the application using the mobile app, try accessing it using the mobile browser.

9.2 ORACLE MOBILE APP HUB

Oracle Mobile Hub is a complete omnichannel platform to help you build, deploy and manage mobile apps that drive engagement with your customers, business partners and employees.

With API approach developers can build compelling web and mobile apps that securely connect to all enterprise systems. It is a cloud-based service that provides a unified hub for developing, deploying, maintaining, monitoring, and analyzing your mobile apps and the resources that they rely on.

Mobile Hub comes with a set of platform APIs that you can use in your apps. You can call these APIs directly from your app code (via client SDK or REST call) and/or from the implementation code of custom APIs.

Available platform APIs includes

- **Offline / Data Sync**: To build applications that cache REST resources for offline use and then synchronize all offline changes
- **Location Services**: To define the user's location using a combination of GPS and Beacons.
- **Push Notifications**: To send notifications to your mobile apps.
- **Storage**: To access the database associated with your Mobile Hub instance.
- **User Management**: Simplifies self-registration and login procedures for the mobile app developer.
- **My Profile**: To retrieve the current app user's profile.
- **SMS** - Integration with Syniverse

You can create your own custom APIs in Mobile Hub to serve the needs of your apps and bots using one or both of the following tools:

- Express API Designer: Enables you to quickly create APIs based on CRUD resources.
- API Designer: Enables you to create or modify an API using the full set of RAML capabilities.

You'll use backends to group the APIs and other resources that your apps and bots need. It provides the security context, meaning that the user has to authenticate through the backend to access those services.

For each backend that you create, you set up how to authenticate with that backend using either one of the following: OAuth, HTTP Basic, SAML/JWT tokens. Browser-based SSO, Facebook Login

Analytics

You can use Oracle Mobile Hub Analytics to gain insight into how (and how often) customers use Applications at any given time. It supports three analytics below:

- **API Calls**: See the number of calls to your app and the response times over various time periods.
- **Events**: The Events report lets you focus on how to improve the mobile app user-experience and how to explore business opportunities.
- **Funnels**: Conversion funnels let you compare how many users start a workflow like a checkout process, user registration process, etc. against how many actually complete it.
- **Users and Sessions**: It shows how many Customers uses a mobile app, where they are located and how long they use

The App Development

Developers are free to choose the front-end development tools and frameworks most suited to their requirements. Any client make REST API can be used

Client SDKs are provided for native app and hybrid developers to make it easier to use APIs and services published from the mobile core.

- Native SDKs: Apple iOS, Android, and Xamarin
- Hybrid & Web SDKs: JavaScript, Apache Cordova

Oracle Visual Builder (VB) is a cloud-based software development Platform as a Service (PaaS) and a hosted environment for your application development infrastructure.

Oracle JavaScript Extension Toolkit (JET) empowers developers by providing a modular open-source toolkit based on modern JavaScript, CSS3 and HTML5 design and development principles.

Source: Oracle Data Sheet

CHAPTER 1

REPORTING IN CLOUD

10.1 INTRODUCTION TO REPORTING IN FUSION APPLICATIONS

There is an extensive need for enterprise reporting in various formats to help the business in getting all the details – from the high-level overview to the transaction level details.

So in this chapter, let us look into these details of how reporting is handled in Fusion Applications.

There are different types of BI output that can be achieved in Fusion Applications:

- BIP Report
- OBIEE
- OTBI Report
- OBIA

A **BIP Report** is very similar to the Business Intelligence Publisher report that is being used in Oracle EBS. This was brought in to move away from the traditional Oracle Reports to a modern technique of extracting data for printing and archiving. This is mostly generated in table format for the past data from the application in different offerings.

OBIEE is Oracle Business Intelligence Enterprise Edition. This was a standalone product installed as the BI Server and integration with Oracle Applications and previously known as BI Answers. It is installed as part of the Fusion Applications middleware suite.

OTBI Report is Oracle Transactional Business Intelligence. OTBI Reports and Analysis provide live data from transactional tables with complex analysis and is seamlessly integrated with Fusion Applications.

OBIA is Oracle Business Intelligence Analytics. Enterprise reporting not only stays within the standard reporting and analysis. For Fusion Applications, the advanced solution based on analysis is embedded within the BI Catalog.

BI Catalog in Fusion Applications

The illustration below shows the Oracle Business Intelligence Catalog.

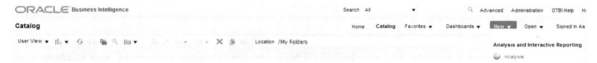

Folder options are highlighted below:

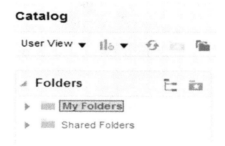

Reports in draft mode and Work in Progress are placed in 'My Folders' and are accessible only by the users. Once the reports are ready to be shared, they are placed in the Shared Folders where any BI user can view/ run the reports.

Various reporting and analysis options are given below.

A new option is used for creating new reports and analysis. Creating a new BI report involves creating a new data model and then a report for layout. Creating a new OTBI report involves creating a new Analysis.

The 'Open' option is used for opening existing reports and analysis.

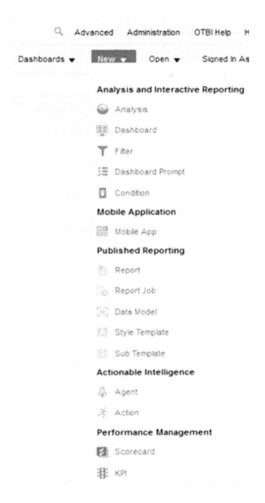

10.2 BI REPORTING IN FUSION APPLICATIONS

BI Publisher reports in Fusion Applications are similar to E-Business Suite in having the data model and layouts separated.

What are the two options for BI Publisher Reports?

☐ Create a new custom BI report using the data model and layout

☐ Seeded BI Publisher reports could be customized to have a custom layout.

The data model has the business logic built into it. It can contain different ways of retrieving data for reporting purposes. The report contains the layout for the data model. There are different types of layouts that can be created in Fusion Applications.

Let us discuss both these options in detail in this chapter.

Custom BI Publisher Report

Custom BIP report can be created in Fusion Applications using the navigation New → Data Model in the 'Reports and Analytics' page as shown below.

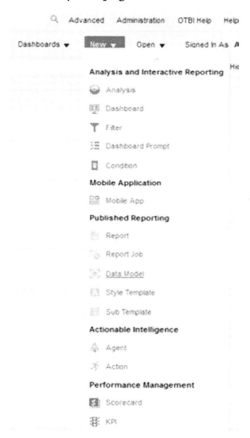

Under the Data Model, six properties are available to be used in building the logic for the report.

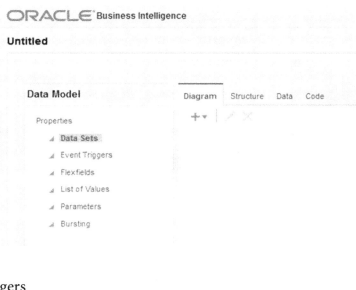

- ☐ Data Sets
- ☐ Event Triggers
- ☐ Flexfields
- ☐ List of Values
- ☐ Parameters
- ☐ Bursting

Data Sets are the code/queries used for extracting the data for the report. They can also be from existing reports or files with data or objects that can be imported.

The most commonly used data set is the 'SQL Query' option where a query can be written to fetch the data as per the reporting requirement. The source can be Financials and SCM (FSCM), HCM Cloud, CRM Cloud or OBIEE.

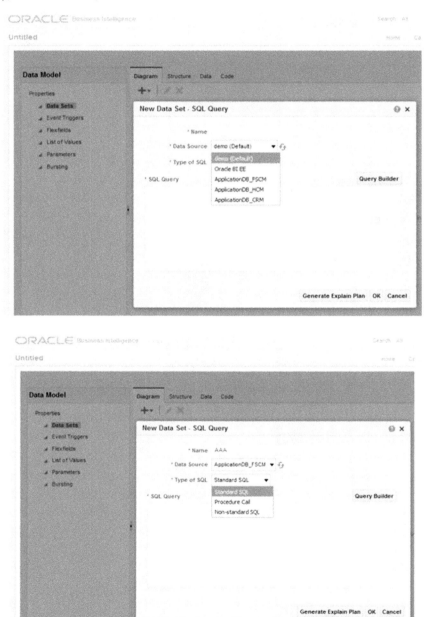

The type of SQL can be Standard, Procedure call or Non-standard SQL. Once the query is formed, click on OK to save it. Also, use the Save option to save the data model under 'My Folders' which is accessible only by the user. Then use the Data option to view the data of the query. The options for the number of records to be viewed are shown below.

Event Triggers: Events triggers are the triggers where business logic can be called before or after execution of the report data model. It can be 'beforeReportTrigger' or 'afterReportTrigger' as shown below.

List of Values: Lists of values are the value sets equivalent of EBS in Fusion Applications. For parameters that require a defined set of values to be displayed for selection, a 'List of Values' is created. It can be created from a SQL Query and then attached to a parameter.

Parameters

Parameters can be defined for the reports. They can be of free text where users can enter any value or they can be of date type that will enable users to choose a date from a calendar. Parameters can be restricted to a certain set of values by attaching a list of values defined in the previous section.

Parameters can be of various types as shown below. To attach a list of values, the type should be chosen as 'Menu'. The particular list of values that has to be attached to the parameter can then be selected from the drop-down menu.

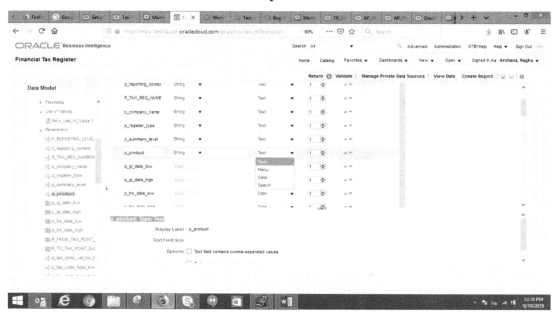

Bursting

Bursting enables the BI Publisher report to be delivered through various means like FTP, email, Printer, Fax, etc. The most common methods are FTP and Email.

Sample code for FTP method of bursting is given below

```
SELECT DISTINCT 'GL' "KEY"
,'Sample Report' TEMPLATE
,'TEXT' OUTPUT_FORMAT
,'SAMPLE_OUTPUT_'||TO_CHAR(SYSDATE,'YYYY-MM-
DD')||TO_CHAR(SYSDATE,'HH24:MI:SS') OUTPUT_NAME
,'GREGORIAN' CALENDAR
,'true' SAVE_OUTPUT
,'FTP' DEL_CHANNEL
,'Host_Name' PARAMETER1
,'/' PARAMETER4
,'SAMPLE_OUTPUT_'||TO_CHAR(SYSDATE,'YYYY-MM-
DD')||TO_CHAR(SYSDATE,'HH24:MI:SS')||'.csv' PARAMETER5
,'true' PARAMETER6
FROM DUAL
```

Report Layout

Create a new Report in Fusion Applications to define a layout for the existing data model. The application requires a sample set of data to be generated for the data model before creating a layout. So it prompts the user to run the data model to generate sample data and save it.

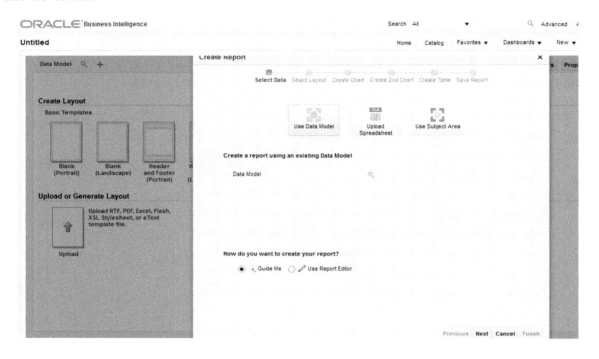

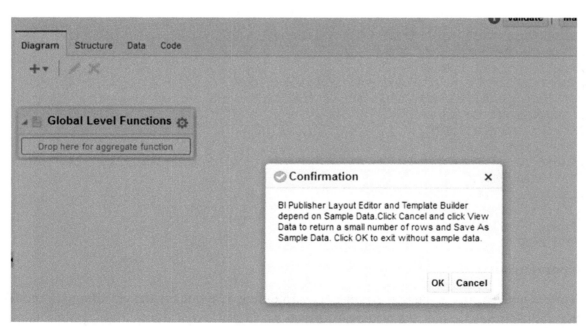

Layouts can be of different types including Excel, RTF, Etext, XSL Stylesheet files that can be uploaded for a specific language. Fusion Applications also have the option of generating the layout based on the columns in the data model. This is the interactive layout where the look & feel of the layout can be modified easily using the editor without having to actually create a layout file as in the case of EBS Applications.

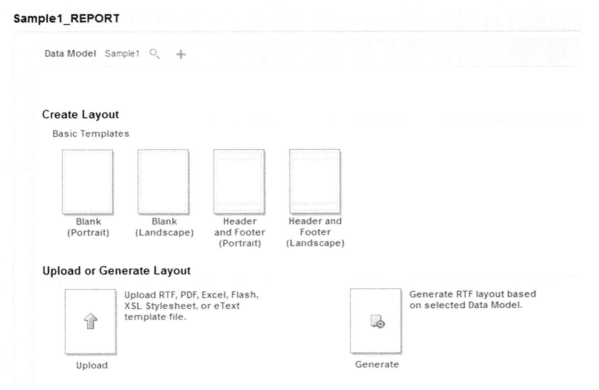

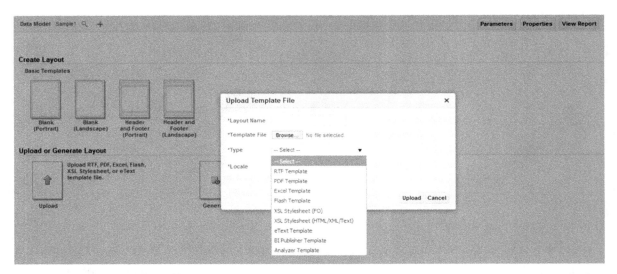

Choosing a simple Blank template would take us to the Interactive layout page where the data model fields would appear to be mapped to the layout. Look & feel can be enhanced using the Layout Grid, Chart, Pivot Table options along with the standard Page break, totals, Page totals, etc.

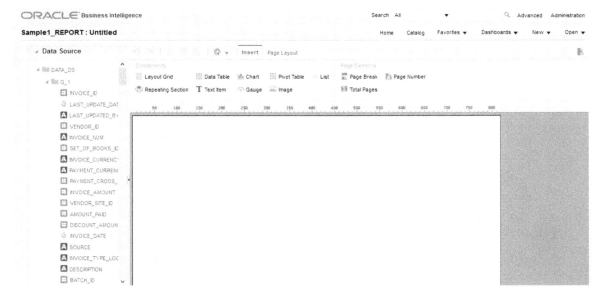

Customizing Standard BI Publisher Report

In Fusion Applications, entire options for reporting are available under the 'Reports and Analytics' page. By default, the seeded reports are available in the folders and subfolders pointing to various offerings in Fusion Applications.

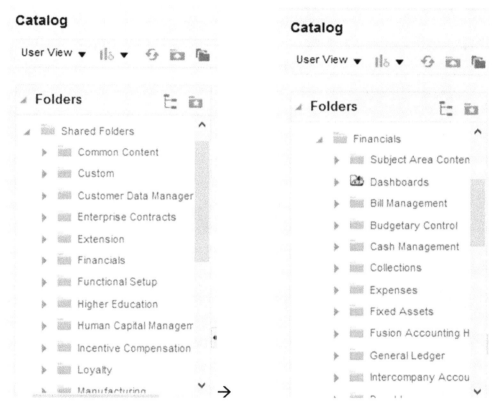

Let us take an example of the standard 'Sales Order Report' and customize this to have a custom layout.

Sales Order Report is available under the navigation Shared Folders -> Supply Chain Management → Order Management → Sales Orders

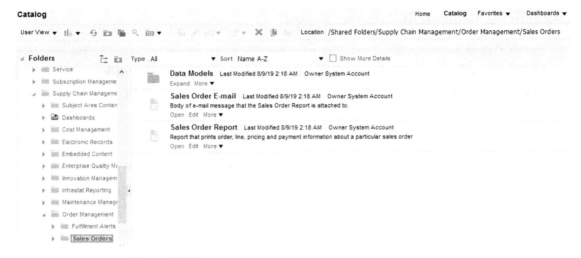

Report properties are shown below:

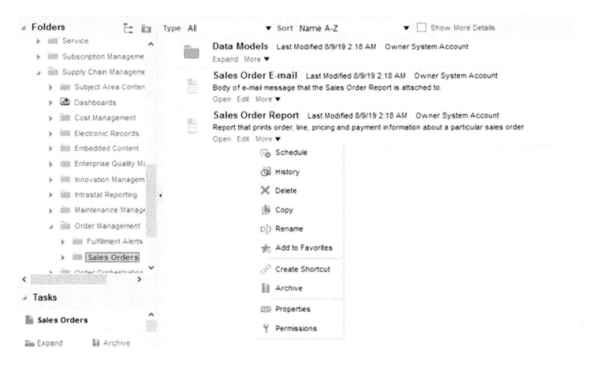

Click on Edit to view the report layout options. The seeded report has the layout below set up as the default layout.

Prepare a new layout in the RTF format. Click on the 'Add New Layout' button to upload a new layout based on the custom requirements.

Once uploaded, the new template will be available in the Template dropdown on the view document dialog. The new template can be flagged as the default template in BI Publisher instead of the seeded template. This will ensure the custom layout is called every time the report is run.

Data Model   Sales Order Report Data Model

Sales Order Report
Edit | Properties | Delete

T2
Edit | Properties | Delete

10.3 OTBI REPORTING IN FUSION APPLICATIONS

Oracle Transactional Business Intelligence (OTBI) is fully integrated with Fusion Applications and does not require any additional system configurations. OTBI can be used as soon as the offerings are configured in Fusion Applications and data is available for reporting. It helps in real-time ad-hoc reporting of the enterprise. Data access and interpretations are easier than before.

OTBI real-time analytics embedded into the Fusion Applications allows users to easily understand the data, filter, sort or drill down, extract data in different formats such as tabular formats or graphical views.

Key Features & Benefits

- Build rich, visual and interactive reports and publish to multiple users.
- Create reports using real-time transactional data
- Easy for business users to analyze, access, use and understand the transactional data.
- Integrates well with the OBIEE features
- Self-service & Ad-hoc analysis
- Enables business in making a better and real-time operational analysis.
- Built-in extensibility to enable business users to adapt the application based on personal or organizational needs.

Security & Roles

OTBI inherits the user roles and security profiles from Fusion Applications. So access to the OTBI subject areas is determined by the Fusion user role. Data that is seen in the OTBI reports are filtered automatically based on the security profile. OTBI supports multi-language translation. The reporting user interface and metadata can switch to your chosen local language. The same report can be deployed in multiple languages across different countries.

OTBI is built using OBIEE which is made of 3 layers – the transactional database layer, then the Physical layer and the Presentation layer. In Fusion Applications, no customizations are possible in the Physical layer unlike in the on-premise implementation of OBIEE where the BI Administrator tool caters to the customizations in the layers.

All the OTBI Subject Areas are suffixed with "Real Time" in the name. Each subject area has one fact folder and several dimension folders. All the OTBI subject areas are secured by Fusion Applications security as it is integrated with the Fusion Applications. Each dimension folder within the subject area is linked with the Fact folder.

Analyses are secured based on the folders in which they are stored. If the Business Intelligence reports are not secured using the report privileges, then they are secured at the folder level by default. Permissions can be set against folders and reports for Application Roles, Catalog Groups or Users.

The following permissions can be set for BI reports:

☐ Read, Write or Execute
☐ Change Permissions
☐ Set Ownership
☐ Run Publisher Report
☐ Schedule Publisher Report
☐ View Publisher Report

Each of the Transaction Analysis Duty roles that grants access to subject areas and Business Intelligence Catalog (BI Catalog) folders inherits one or more Reporting Data Duty roles. These duty roles grant access to the data.

Custom job roles can also be created to grant access to the OTBI reports. Assign the Oracle Transactional Business Intelligence duty roles to these custom job roles as needed. These transaction analysis duty roles ensure that the custom job role has the function and data security for running the reports.

Business Intelligence Roles apply to both Oracle BI Publisher (BIP) and Oracle Fusion Transactional Business Intelligence (OTBI). Access is granted through these roles for the business intelligence functionality to run or create reports. BI roles are defined as application roles in Oracle Entitlements Server and are listed below.

☐ BI Consumer Role → Access to run BI Reports
☐ BI Author Role → Access to create and edit Reports
☐ BI Administrator Role → Access to perform administrative tasks like creating and editing dashboards and handling security permissions
☐ BI Publisher Data Model Developer Role → Access to create and edit Oracle BI Publisher data models.

How to View Permissions of OTBI Reports?

To view the permissions for the OTBI reports, a role that inherits BI Administrator Role should be assigned.

☐ Navigator → Tools → Reports and Analytics
☐ Content pane → Browse Catalog → BI Catalog page opens

- Folders pane → Shared Folders → Financials → Fixed Assets → Additions → List of reports appear
- Under the reports → Click on More → Permissions → Permissions Dialog Box Opens

Generating OTBI Reports

Oracle Transactional Business Intelligence (OTBI) reports can be created using the following data sources.

- ☐ Data Model
- ☐ Spreadsheet
- ☐ Subject Area

For example, to analyze journal data, 'General Ledger – Journals Real Time' subject area can be used as a source to generate a report in the required layout.

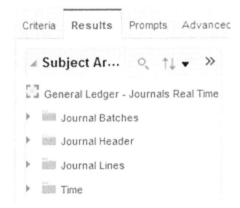

Data Structure for Analytics

The BI repository contains the metadata that defines the columns which can be included in the analyses and the source of the data. The repository is organized into subject areas that contain folders with the columns.

The 3 types of columns are given below

Fact → Measure of a value (numbers)

Attributes → Piece of information about a business object; Example: Start Date

Hierarchy → Data values organized hierarchically; Example: Year, Quarter, Month

A subject area contains the columns related to a business object or area. When the analysis is created, the subject area is first chosen and then the folders within the subject area are opened to include the columns required. Each subject area has one fact folder and several dimension folders. Folders can also have subfolders. Fact folders contain fact columns and are usually placed at the bottom of the list of folders. Dimension folders contain attribute and hierarchical columns and are joined to the fact folder within the subject area. Analysis can have columns from multiple subject areas.

Create and Edit Analyses using Wizard

The function of a wizard is to guide in creating or editing analyses. Oracle Business Intelligence Answers can be used to create dashboards and to delete analyses.

Create Analyses

- Open Reports and Analytics pane in the work area
- Click on Create and select Analysis
- Select the subject area that has the columns required for the report.
- Additional subject areas can also be added if required.
- Select the columns to be included in the report and click on Next
- Enter the title for the analysis if required
- Select the type of layout for the analysis – table of graphical and click on Next
- Additional options for sorting, filtering and formatting are also available if required.
- Click on Finish to save the Analysis and enter a Name.
- Click on Submit.

Edit Analyses

- Open Reports and Analytics pane in the work area
- Select the Analysis in the pane and click Edit
- Perform the editing based on the options discussed in the previous section.
- To update an existing Analysis, select the same name in the same folder.
- Click on Submit

10.4 DASHBOARDS IN FUSION APPLICATIONS

Introduction

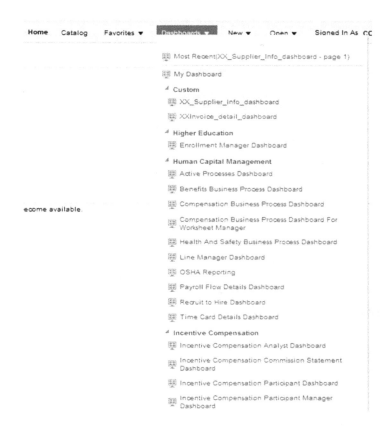

The dashboard is a way of displaying personalized information through different views like Pie-Charts, Bars and Graphs as business required. It is possible to create or edit dashboards via Manage Dashboard privilege, which is managed by the administrator.

My Dashboard, a personalized view, is a dashboard page that you create and save as your default.

The dashboard consists of one or more pages which include the following:

The results of the analysis: An analysis can be shown in various views, such as a table, graph, and gauge. Users can examine and analyze results, print as PDF or HTML, save as PDF, or export them to a spreadsheet.), Images, Text, Oracle BI Publisher reports

The screenshots below gives pre-configured dashboards. The ones starting with XX are the custom dashboards and all the others are standard ones.

Sample Dashboard

Dashboard Builder and Objects

We use the Dashboard builder to add and edit pages in a dashboard. The Dashboard Builder is composed of the following:

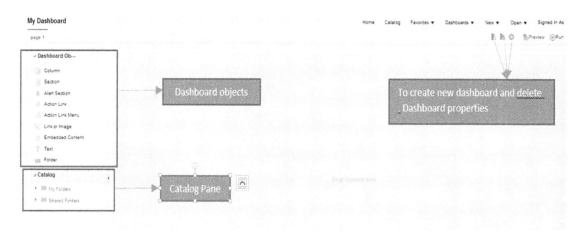

- **Dashboard Toolbar:**

  The toolbar allows you to perform tasks such as adding or deleting pages, previewing, saving, and so on. In the Dashboard Toolbar, the Tools toolbar button provides options to set dashboard properties, set page report links, and so on.

- **Dashboard Objects pane:**

  Items that are used only in a dashboard. Examples of dashboard objects are sections to hold content, action links, and embedded content that is displayed in a frame on a dashboard

- **Catalog pane:**

  Items that are saved to the Catalog: for example, Analysis, Prompts, Reports and so on. In a dashboard, the results of an analysis can be shown in various views, such as a table, graph, and gauge. (The results of an analysis are the output that is returned from the Oracle BI Server that matches the analysis criteria.) Users can examine and analyze results, save or print them, or download them to a spreadsheet.

- **Page Layout pane:**

  This is a workspace that holds your objects, which are displayed on the dashboard.

  Every dashboard has at least one page, which can be empty. Dashboard pages are identified by tabs across the top of the dashboard. Multiple pages are used to organize content.

☐ **Columns** are used to align content on a dashboard.

☐ **Sections** are used within columns to hold the content, such as action links, analysis, and so on. It can be dragged and dropped as many sections as needed to a column.

☐ **Alert Section** is used to add a section in which we can display Alerts from Agents. We can add an Alert section to an additional dashboard page so that the section will then appear on multiple dashboard pages.

☐ **Text** is used to include Text to the dashboard using Text object in Dashboard objects.

☐ **Link or Image** is used to include a URL to another BI or OTBI report or images.

Steps to create a Dashboard

☐ Create a new analysis showing invoice amount against each Business unit with an Accounting period as a prompted parameter (This can be used in the dashboard as a column prompt).

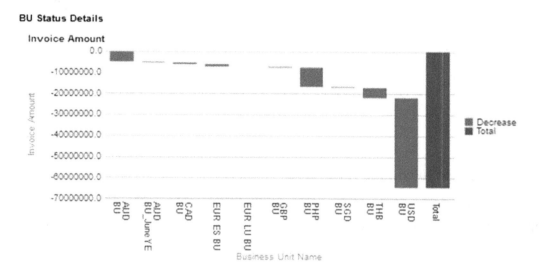

Create a dashboard

Click on My Dashboard in the panel and it will direct to the Dashboard page.

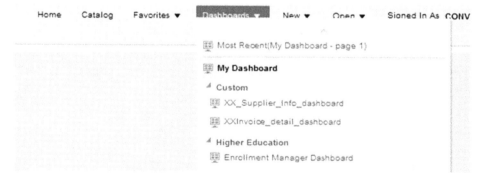

Click on "Edit" button in below screen to go to the Dashboard builder page.

Embed content in the dashboard page

In below Dashboard builder page you can see the list of contents that can be dragged and dropped into the page layout section.

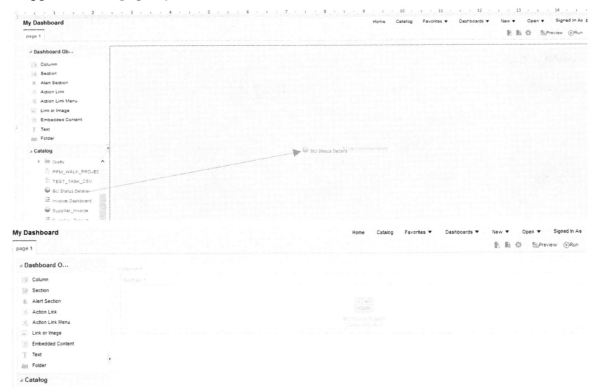

Create a dashboard prompt

A dashboard prompt is a special filter that filters analysis data and the same can be added in a dashboard.

There are two prompt types

Named Prompts:

Named prompts will always appear on the dashboard page so that the user can select different values without having to rerun the dashboard. These prompts will be stored in the catalog for reuse.

Inline prompts:

Inline prompts are included in an analysis and are not stored in the Catalog.

To create a Dashboard prompt use Navigation below.

Select the required subject area and choose a field that we used for embedded analysis.

Now the prompt can be dragged in the dashboard page view.

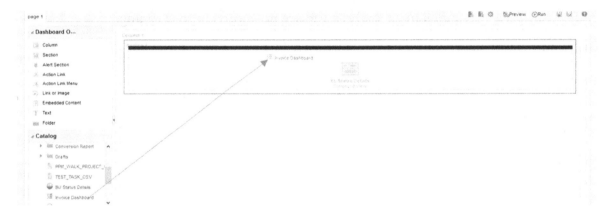

We can use "Link or Image" objects to land into the required page from the dashboard.

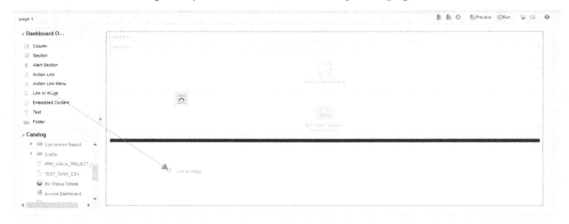

Link or Image Properties

In the dashboard below, the link is given to redirect to the home page.

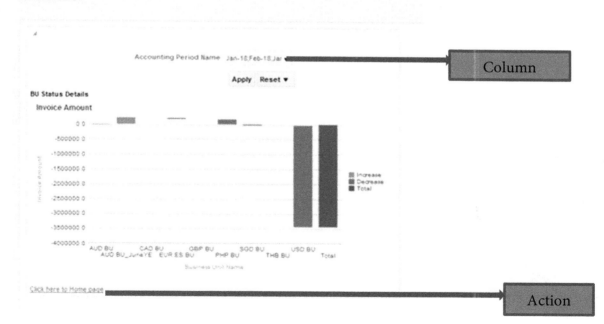

PERSONALIZATIONS IN FUSION APPLICATIONS

11.1 PERSONALIZATION THROUGH SANDBOX

Introduction

In this blog, we will try to understand what is meant by the Customization layer in the context of Fusion Cloud Application and also try to understand how does customization layers ensure that the correct customizations or personalizations are available at run time to appropriate users.

There are built-in customization layers in your application to make customizations that affect only certain instances or users of an application. Before we create customizations, we should select the layer in which we want to customize. Most of the customization tools provide a dialog box for selecting the layer for your customizations.

Built-In Customization Layers

The customization layers available to an application depend on its application family. However, all applications have the following customization layers:

- Site layer: Customizations made in the site layer affect all users.
- User layer: All personalizations are made in the user layer. Users don't have to explicitly select this layer as it's automatically applied while personalizing the application.

Layer Hierarchy

The layers are applied in a hierarchy, and the highest layer in that hierarchy in the current context is considered the tip layer. With the default customization layers, the user layer is the tip layer. An object may be customized more than once, but in different layers. At run time, the tip-layer customizations take precedence. For example, say you customize in the site layer. You use Page Composer to add a region on a page. A user personalizes the same page to hide the region. In such a case, the user-layer customization takes precedence for that user at run time.

Storage of Customizations and Layer Information

Customizations aren't saved to the base standard artifact. Instead, they're saved in Extensible Markup Language (XML) files for each layer. These files are stored in an Oracle Metadata Services (MDS) repository. The XML file acts like a list of instructions that determines how the artifact looks or behaves in the application, based on the customization layer. The customization engine in MDS manages this process.

When you apply an application patch or upgrade, it updates the base artifacts, but it doesn't touch the customizations stored in XML files. The base artifact is replaced. Hence, when you run the application after the patch or upgrade, the XML files are layered on top of the new version. You don't need to redo your customizations.

Example

For example, the Sales application has a layer for the job roles. When you customize an artifact, you can choose to make that customization available only to users with a specific role, for example, a sales representative.

We would not be making any changes to the pages but rather try to understand the effect customization layer has on a specific application page from a conceptual point of view.

Let's say for this example we want to remove the Quick Create panel from the Sales home page, and customize this page only for users with the Sales Representative role.

The perquisites for this are as follows:

☐ Availability of an Active Sandbox

We would need to activate a sandbox (shown below).

Login to Application with appropriate credentials (HCM_IMPL in this case)

Click on 'Customize Pages' link

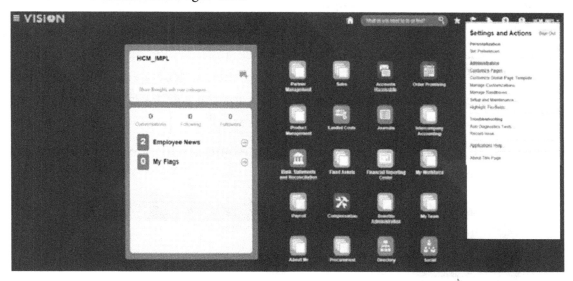

A popup message box would appear stating that a Sandbox must be activated to perform customizations

Next, we need to click on the 'Activate Sandbox' button, choose one of the available sandboxes (which would appear on a new popup window and choose the 'Active' button)

The sandbox will be activated (horizontal strip would appear on top of the screen with the name of the sandbox mentioned)

☐ Appropriate Job Role

When you customize a page for a specific job role that job role must be assigned to you for you to test the customization in the sandbox. Your security administrator can either assign the job role to you directly, or make the job role self-requestable for you to add it yourself from the resource directory.

☐ Selection of Customization Layer

Select the layer in which you want to make your customization. In this case, select the role layer with the value, Sales Representative. While customizing, when you remove the panel from the page, an XML file is generated. This file contains instructions to remove the panel, but only for the role layer, and only when the value is Sales Representative.

Note: HCM_IMPL does not have the Sales Administrator Job Role attached to the user and hence not displayed.

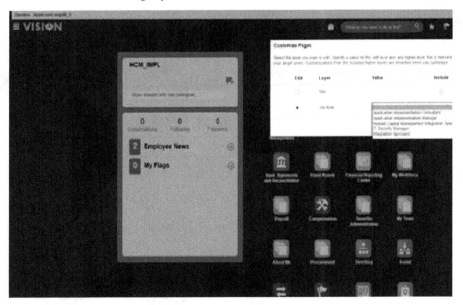

So these three are the perquisites for this example.

The customization engine in MDS then stores the XML file in an MDS repository.

When someone signs in and requests an artifact, the customization engine in MDS checks the repository for XML files matching the artifact and the given context. On matching, the customization engine layers the instructions on top of the base artifact.

In this example, whenever someone:

With the role of Sales Representative (the context) requests the Sales home page (the artifact), before the page is rendered, the customization engine in MDS:

☐ Pulls the corresponding XML file from the repository

☐ Layers it on top of the standard Sales home page

☐ Removes the panel

Without the role of Sales Representative signs in, the customization engine doesn't layer the XML file on top of the standard Sales home page. So, the Quick Create panel is displayed on the page.

Personalization

All users of the application can use the Personalization menu items to personalize certain pages.

For example, you can:

☐ Move elements around on a page

☐ Hide elements

☐ Add available elements to a page

While you personalize a page, the customization engine in MDS creates an XML file specific to a user (in this case, you), for the user layer.

For example, say User 1 (with the role of Sales Representative) personalizes the Sales home page. An XML file, noting the changes that the user made, is stored in the repository.

When User 1 signs in, the customization engine in MDS:

☐ Pulls the XML file with the sales representative customizations from the repository, and layers the file on top of the standard Sales home page.

☐ Pulls the XML file with User 1 personalization's, thus enabling the user to see the personalization changes along with the Sales Representative Changes.

11.2 CUSTOMIZING LOOK AND FEEL OF FUSION APPLICATIONS

MODIFYING THE LOOK AND FEEL OF FUSION APPLICATION

The topic for discussion appears self-explanatory but in case it doesn't let me try and help all the readers. Fusion Applications has a specific look and feel (skin color, background/foreground color of its page, logo on the first page).

This article will try to explore and showcase a scenario where we could try to change some of the seeded attributes and at this point, it makes sense to understand the advantages/need/use for making such changes and why should we rather spend our time and energy on making some changes. Some of the salient points justifying such a move are:

☐ Company-Specific Logo on Welcome Page

Each company prefers to have its own logo on the Welcome Page instead of the seeded one delivered by Oracle. While on one hand it does help individuals to identify the Environment that they are working, on the other hand it also does a bit on the advertisement part. No harm displaying the company logo on the ERP application being used by the company.

☐ Adhering to a specific color

While Oracle has tried its level best to present the application in the most pleasant way carefully choosing the background and foreground colors, some companies might decide to have a different shade on their environment. The application provides flexibility and enables users to do so.

☐ Uniquely identify a particular instance (POD / Fusion Environment

For a typical organization using Fusion Applications or for that matter any other ERP system there are multiple environments (Also referred to as Instances / Pods) like Development, UAT, SIT, Pre-Production and Production.

Since all of the above looks similar at times it becomes difficult to identify the Environment on which a specific task is being carried out. A change supposed to be done on Development Environment may be performed on UAT or vice versa and this might cause issues.

One smart way of avoiding such mistakes would be using smart color-coding scheme on the environment (maybe as displayed below):

Environment Name	Color
Development	Green
UAT	Yellow
SIT	Blue
Pre-Production	Gold
Production	Orange

There could be many more reasons but for now, we would restrict ourselves to the above three and continue with our example.

Example: In this example, we would change the logo from the seeded one (VISION as displayed in the first screenshot) and replace the same with a new logo (customer-specific one).

As a first step, we have to log in to the application (specific Fusion POD where we intend to make the changes) and click on the 'Appearance' (under Tools menu) hyper-link

This takes us to the following screen:

Logo

Edit Button

Once you click on the Edit button you would be asked to activate a sandbox (this feature ensures that all the changes are made in a specific customized area ensuring that in case something does not go well the changes can be reverted)

We already have a sandbox "ApplcoreLongSB_01" and we will use the same here instead of creating a new sandbox.

Once the same is set as Active you would notice the same displayed on the topmost region (snap-shot below)

We need to click on the 'Update' button and point to our logo/image (in this example we have used an image which is stored in a local machine but this could very well be an online image too).

Next, we should click on 'OK' button followed by the 'Apply' button.

This change will appear on all the pages and the same could be verified too by navigating to different Fusion pages. In this example, we will verify the same on the homepage to get a confirmation.

One important point to note here is that all these changes did not require a downtime and were on the go which is a big plus and very good feature to have.

We are on the homepage now and it would be hard to miss that the logo has been changed to the new one

Although we have already made the change in the logo the change is too small and so to make the change simple and clearly visible let us try to change the background color too. We would change the same to ED6A24 (for this example).

Background color changed to ED6A24

And once we click on 'Apply' we are able to view the change:

And finally a look at the Homepage:

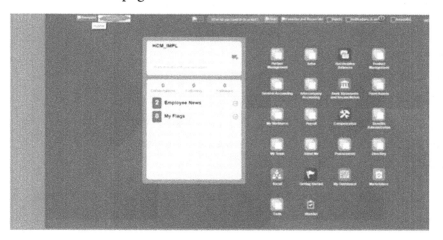

So we have now seen how easily we are able to change the appearance of a Fusion Environment and we may change the skin, theme and various colors available. Each one of the same can be tried and verified by using the same process and hopefully, you all would be able to get desired results.

Oracle BPM Worklist enables business users to access and act on tasks assigned to them. For example, from a Worklist, a loan agent can review loan applications or a manager can approve employee vacation requests.

Oracle BPM Worklist provides different functionality based on the user profile. Standard user profiles include task assignee, supervisor, process owner, reviewer, and administrator. For example, Worklist users can update payloads or business data, attach documents or comments, and route tasks to other users, in addition to completing tasks by providing conclusions such as approvals or rejections. Supervisors or group administrators can use the Worklist to analyze tasks assigned to a group and route them appropriately.

Using Oracle BPM Worklist, task assignees can do the following:

- Perform authorized actions on tasks in the Worklist, acquire and check out shared tasks, define personal to-do tasks, and define subtasks.
- Filter tasks in a Worklist view based on various criteria.
- Work with standard work queues, such as high priority tasks, tasks due soon, and so on. Work queues allow users to create a custom view to group a subset of tasks in the Worklist, for example, high priority tasks, tasks due in 24 hours, expense approval tasks, and more.
- Define custom work queues.
- Gain proxy access to part of another user's Worklist.
- Define custom vacation rules and delegation rules.
- Enable group owners to define task dispatching rules for shared tasks.
- Collect a complete workflow history and audit trail.
- Use digital signatures for tasks."

Now we see how Approval Management (AME) is different from Oracle EBS and Fusion Instances.

BPM IMPLEMENTATION IN FUSION APPLICATIONS

12.1 MANAGING APPROVALS IN EBS

☐ About AME:

Oracle Approvals Management (AME) enables you to define business rules governing the process for approving transactions in Oracle applications that have integrated AME.

☐ Integration of AME with Oracle E-Business Suite Application

INTEGRATING APPLICATION	INTEGRATING APPLICATION
Service Work in Process	Quoting Enterprise Asset Management
Service Contracts	Payables
Field Service	Inventory
Partner Management	Receivables
Purchase Requisition	Receivables
Payroll	Work In Process

☐ Business Flow

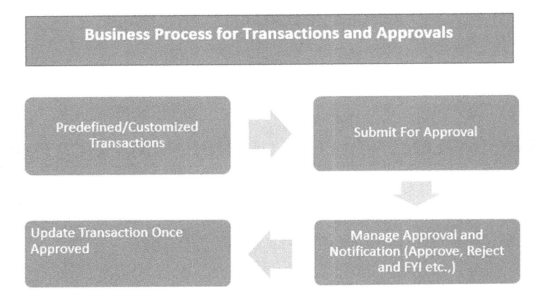

☐ Structure of AME

AME is a framework of well-defined approval rules constructed using the following 5 components for a given transaction type:

☐ Transaction Type:

A transaction type describes the type of transaction for which business rules and approval routings will be based. Examples of transaction types are:

☐ Purchase Requisition Approval (Purchasing)
☐ Requester Change Order Approval (Purchasing)
☐ Service contract Approval (service contract)
☐ Work Order Approval (EAM)

A Transaction type is a combination of Rules, Attributes, Conditions and Approval Groups.

Please see the screenshot below:

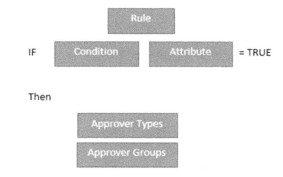

☐ Attributes

Attributes within AME are business variables that represent the value of a data element of a given transaction.

- • Attributes in AME can be created as being static or they can be dynamic in nature
- • Attributes can be defined at 3 different levels – Header, Line Item and Cost Center level.
- • Examples of attributes are:
  - ☐ Contract_Amount (service contracts)
  - ☐ Request_Severity (service Request)
  - ☐ Item_Number (Purchasing)

☐ Conditions

Conditions are used to evaluate the value of attributes in a particular transaction

➤ The "Condition" component tells AME engine to trigger an AME rule if the result of the Condition is TRUE
➤ One or more attributes are used to define a condition.
   o Actions
   - 'Actions' describes what should be done in AME if a particular condition is satisfied by the transaction
   - Action Type is a collection of actions having similar functionality. Every action belongs to an action type.

Action Types	
Job Based	Absolute Job Level
	Final Approver Only
	Manager then Final Approver
	Relative Job Level
	Supervisory Level
HR Position Based	HR Position
	HR Position Level
Approver Group Based	Pre-Chain-of-authority approvals
	Post-chain-of-authority approvals
	Approval-group chain of authority

➤ Approver Groups

Approver Group is used to fetch approvers from Oracle Applications (HRMS).

- Static or Dynamic in nature
- The voting method determines the order in which the Group Members are notified and also how the decision of the group's approval.

➤ Rules

Transforms the business rules into approval rules to specify approvers in the transaction's approval list

- Rules can also be categorized as "FYI" or "Approval".
- A rule is constructed using the following components:
  1. Rule Type
  2. Item Class
  3. Category
  4. Conditions
  5. Actions

12.2 MANAGING APPROVALS IN FUSION APPLICATIONS

Oracle Business Process Management (BPM):

The BPM Worklist Application is a web-based application that lets users access tasks assigned to them and perform actions based on their roles in the approval process. Administrators can set up approval groups and task level configuration via an administration portal or through the Oracle BPM Worklist.

As in EBS suite we have different types of transactions ("**Purchase Requisition Approval**") we have tasks defined for each Transaction in Fusion for example for I-Expenses the task is "**Manage Expense Approvals**" and for Procurement the task is "**Manage Requisition Approvals**".

How to configure or edit Manage Requisition Approval process:

Navigate to: Setup and Maintenance > Select: Procurement > Setup button > Functional Areas: procurement> Show: All Tasks > Manage Requisition Approvals > Oracle BPM Worklist as shown below

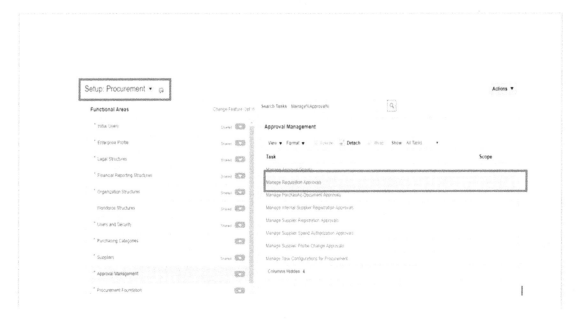

Click on the Manage Requisition Approvals which will take you to Manage Requisition Approval Set up page as shown below:

You can create new rules by clicking the Edit Rules button as shown in the above screenshot or by selecting create option from Actions Drop Down.

An approval rule is composed of the following:

☐ Rule Name

☐ Condition

☐ Action

Rule Name: The Rule Name is used to identify the approval rule.

☐ In cases where there are large numbers of rules, users can filter search results in the Query by Example fields.

Condition: The Condition indicates when the approval rule will be applied.

A rule can contain multiple conditions, and you can select the "and" or "or" operators to indicate if all conditions in the approval rule must be true or if only one condition must be true for the approval rule to apply.

For example, if the requisition amount is less than 10,000 and requisitioning BU is US Business Unit. A condition can be defined using attributes seeded in a dimension or user-defined attributes. Please look into the section on how to create User Defined Attributes.

You can create the condition by using predefined Approval Task attributes or by using User Defined Attributes.

You can search for any standard attributes and can create the condition as shown below.

Action: An action defines what needs to be done if the conditions of a rule are met.

It identifies if approvals or FYI notifications are required and the type of users needed to approve or receive notification for a document.

The supported action types are: -

- Approval required
- Approval actions required from the recipients of the approval tasks - Automatic
- Automatically approve or reject the approval task - Information only
- FYI notifications sent to recipients

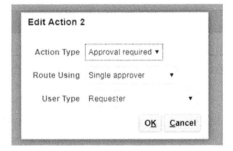

In the screenshot below you can see we created Action based on Condition

The Supported Routing Methods are:

- Approval Group

☐ Job-Level
☐ Position Hierarchy
☐ Single Approver
☐ Supervisory Hierarchy

User-Defined Attributes

Organizations have different requirements for document approvals. Some of these requirements may include the need to perform currency conversions for amount based attributes, or derive approvers based on roll-up amounts across lines within a document with common attributes. These user-defined attributes are managed and used within a specific approval task.

There are two types of user-defined attributes they are:

☐ Currency-Based
☐ Summation.

Currency-Based User-Defined Attributes:

You can define currency-based attributes such that amounts in different currencies are converted to a specific currency for rule evaluation.

For example, Acme Corp. creates an attribute "USD Requisition Amount" and uses the attribute for rule conditions, such as if the USD Requisition Amount is less than 500, approvals from the preparer's manager is required and so forth. If a requisition created in Mexico is submitted, where the functional currency is pesos, the requisition amount will first be converted to USD before rules are evaluated.

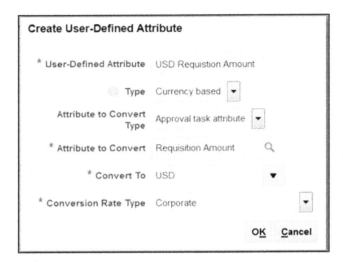

Summation User-Defined Attributes: Customers who need to perform approval routings based on data aggregated across one or more attributes when a document contains more than one line, schedule or distribution can create summation user-defined attributes.

For example, Acme Corp's approval policy requires the number of IT approvers to be based on the total amount of IT requests within a requisition. If the total IT amount is less than 1200 USD, then the IT manager needs to approve. If the IT amount exceeds 1200 USD, then the IT manager, director and VP need to approve the document.

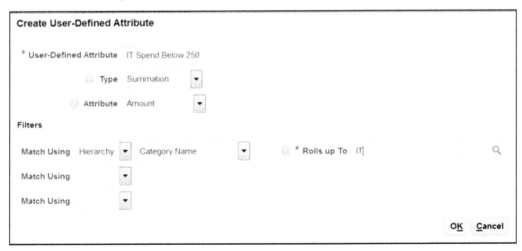

Deploying Approval Rules: Any changes made to the rules or any rules that have been newly added have to be deployed for them to be effective.

- ☐ Deploying approval rules will require users to click on the Deploy button on the Edit Rules and on the Manage Approval Rules page.
- ☐ If users do not intend to deploy the changes that were made to the rules, they can choose to click on the
- ☐ Discard button to revert the rules to the last deployed state.

Save: Save or Save and Close will save the updated rules to the database without deploying them. Users can edit and save rules across multiple participants before deploying them.

Deploy: Deploy updates the rules engine and makes all the rule changes across all participants effective. It is displayed on both the Manage Approval Rules page and the Edit Rules page. The Deploy button is disabled by default and is enabled when there are rules that have been setting up Document Approvals updated and saved.

Discard: Discard is displayed on both the Manage Approval Rules page and the Edit Rules page. It is disabled by default and is enabled when there are rules that have been updated and saved. Discard removes any rule changes that were saved and the rules will go back to the last deployed state.

Once You Click on Deploy The below warning Message will Appear.

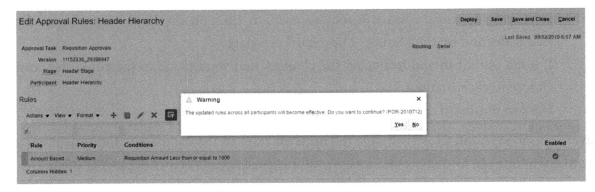

Click on the Confirmation Dialog Message.

Once the changes are deployed, the rule will be effective once by enabling (Enable) button adjacent to the "Edit" button where you created or edited the rule as shown below.

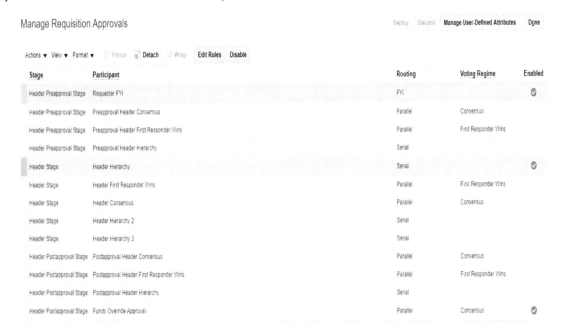

KEY CONSIDERATIONS BEFORE CLOUD MIGRATION

There can be "n" number of key issues that need to be taken into consideration when developing a cloud strategy. Addressing these issues at the early stages can save a significant amount of time.

Below are some key considerations which need to be considered before starting or migrating to Cloud.

DATA: One of the primary considerations is Data. Before making a decision about whether to migrate applications it is vital to understand where the data will be held and can be transferrable.

Note that as stated in the Oracle Cloud Hosting and Delivery Policies, as well as Oracle's Services Privacy Services, Oracle Cloud services are in alignment with the ISO/IEC 27001:2005 security standards and also adhere to the Safe Harbor Privacy Principles of notice, choice, onward transfer, security, data integrity, access, and enforcement. In addition, the Oracle Cloud has been awarded Trustee's Privacy Seal.

Our recommendation is to adopt a three-stage approach.

The first stage is to conduct a data discovery exercise to identify the sources of the organization's most critical data entities. In parallel, cloud and data architects should collaborate to define a common data model that can be used in the second and third stages.

In the second stage, data is extracted from the identified Legacy systems into an intermediate system, where it is normalized and cleaned, removing duplicates, redundancy, and outdated information.

The third stage involves the creation of another intermediate system that is used to load the cleaned data into the target SaaS system. One factor that is often overlooked is the complexity of loading the data. SaaS APIs can be very complex so it is vital that whoever undertakes the migration has a sound knowledge of how these work and, ideally that will save time and effort.

CONSOLIDATION: Adopting cloud services offers plenty of opportunities for consolidating both applications and hardware, which can significantly reduce administration, maintenance, and support costs.

SECURITY: One of the key benefits of migrating enterprise applications to the cloud is that they typically allow companies to quickly and easily make them available in multiple locations and geographies, and on various mobile devices. As a result, organizations can empower employees to be more productive, collaborate better with partners and suppliers, and provide new services to customers.

However, all these benefits also have security implications.

In putting together a cloud migration strategy, organizations should consider the security of:

- ☐ The service provider's data center. However, with any reputable service provider this should not be a problem.
- ☐ The network between the service providers and their company locations.
- ☐ Devices carrying by employees.
- ☐ Customer access to web applications/Portals.

Security (36%), cloud computing (31%) and mobile devices (28%) are the top 3 initiatives IT executives are planning to have their organizations focus on over the next 12 months. Source: 2015 State of the Network Study

As stated earlier the Oracle Cloud complies with several regulatory requirements, such as the ISO/IEC 27001:2005 security standards and Safe Harbor.

Read the Oracle Cloud Hosting and Delivery Policies and the Oracle's Services Privacy Services for further information.

INTEGRATION: To provide a seamless user experience applications will need to be integrated. Careful consideration needs to be given to the technologies to achieve this. As discussed earlier, we would recommend using Oracle PaaS (Integration/SOA Cloud Services) and Oracle SOA Suite 12c for on-premise integrations. Plus, it's vitally important to have a thorough understanding of the Oracle cloud solutions being adopted and how they integrate, what Integration Cloud Service (ICS) connectors are available, what APIs from the fusion apps enterprise repository can be used, and what limitations apply when consuming these APIs.

IMPLEMENTATION: One of the promises of Oracle Cloud solutions is that they are quick and easy to implement and this is certainly true if a single application is being implemented from scratch in isolation. However, as we saw in the data section above, there is rather more to implementing an integrated cloud strategy. In fact, around 50% of all cloud adoptions fail due to issues related to integration, data migration, or SaaS customizations. Vendors such as Oracle impose restrictions on how their products are configured, customized, extended and as previously mentioned, integrated. So unless companies are fully aware of these constraints and how to implement Oracle PaaS to deliver customizations, extensions, and integrations – such as Java Cloud Service for SaaS Extensions, Process Cloud Service, and Integration Cloud Service (amongst other cloud services) - the chances are they will encounter issues during or after adoption. Consequently, companies will want to consider carefully whether they want to 'do it alone' or whether it makes sense to partner with an organization that has developed tools and accelerators to help with the implementation process.

FUSION IMPLEMENTATION APPROACH

The typical Fusion implementation looks like below and it has mostly 5 phases.

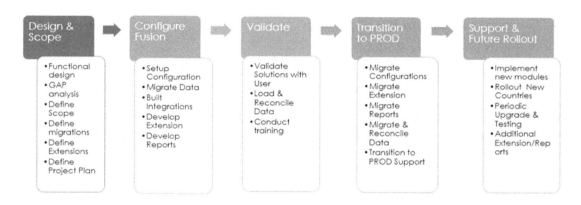

- [ ] Design and Scope
  - o Functional design
  - o GAP analysis
  - o Define Scope
  - o Define migrations
  - o Define Extensions
  - o Define Project Plan
- [ ] Configurations
  - o Setup Configuration

- o Migrate Data
- o Built Integrations
- o Develop Extension
- o Develop Reports
- ☐ Validate
  - o Validate Solutions with User
  - o Load & Reconcile Data
  - o Conduct training
- ☐ Transition to PROD
  - o Migrate Configurations
  - o Migrate Extension
  - o Migrate Reports
  - o Migrate & Reconcile Data
  - o Transition to PROD Support
- ☐ Support and Future Rollout
  - o Implement new modules
  - o Rollout New Countries
  - o Periodic Upgrade & Testing
  - o Additional Extension/Reports

Cloud Migration – Key Considerations

- ☐ Organizational Fitment to Cloud Functionality
- ☐ Historical Data and Data volume to be Converted
- ☐ Integration Requirements with 3rd Party and exiting EBS
- ☐ Standardization of Processes, Consider your existing RICE Objects
- ☐ Scope of Migration
- ☐ BI/Reporting Layer
- ☐ Present and change in System Architecture

Many customers elect to perform a phased approach to their cloud migration to ensure that core business processes are not negatively affected by the migration.

Implementation Best practices

The implementation can be done with any of the below 3 scenarios:

- ☐ Big Bang Financials, SCM and HCM are implemented at the same time.
- ☐ Financials, SCM and HCM (Phased) Financials is implemented first then SCM second and HCM are implemented in a future phase.
- ☐ HCM, Financials and SCM (Phased) HCM is implemented first then Financials and SCM are implemented in a future phase.

Generally Financials, SCM and HCM solutions were implemented across multiple database instances, which required additional point integrations to facilitate configuration and transaction sharing. With Oracle Financials, SCM and HCM cloud services, you have a single data model that eliminates a majority of point integrations. However, because of this tight integration model, it is important that you consider key configuration decisions across the enterprise solution, regardless of your specific implementation project scope.

Where to Start

There are no barriers to start with any Oracle Cloud Pillar. Oracle's Functional Setup Manager has the ability to identify the dependencies regardless of starting with either HCM, SCM or Financials.

Customer Business Model			Map to Oracle Cloud		Impact Analaysis
Funcitonal Area	Activity	Role/Title	Feature	User Profile	Description
Catalog Management	Catalog Item Creation	Item Manager	Add and maintain items	Item Master Manager	Need to update policies/procedures for Item Master Managers
Vendor/eSupplier	Procurement and Payables Adminstrator adds/maintains qualified suppliers	Supplier Manager	Add and maintains vendors	Supplier Manager	eSupplier/setup portal for suppliers/new policies and procedures; training of new suppliers for self-service
Purchasing	Indirect Requisition	35 Account Planners and Inventory Analysis	Manual Requisition for Items	Purchasing Agent	Requires policy changes/training given that the process is now automated
Supply Planning	Direct Requisition	Account Planner	Planning Requisition	Planning Requester	As part of the rollout a new policy will be in place to limit account planner access certain preferred suppliers. Exceptions will be handled manually

Fit/Gap Analysis This exercise to compare how the existing organization's structure aligns with the Oracle Fusion cloud services delivered roles and responsibilities. This will also help quantify the organizational change required for successful implementation and provide insight into the potential role mappings that may need to be performed in managing role mappings

Defining Enterprise Configurations

Oracle Fusion Cloud provides a series of tools to guide and support you during this most important step in your implementation. Below are some of the tools available

- Enterprise Structures Configurator - to simulate and finalize core enterprise structures across.
- Implementation Templates - used to complete configuration setup to support the implementation scope defined in FSM
- File-Based/HCM Data Loader – loading a large number of values for a configuration

Enterprise Structures Configurator

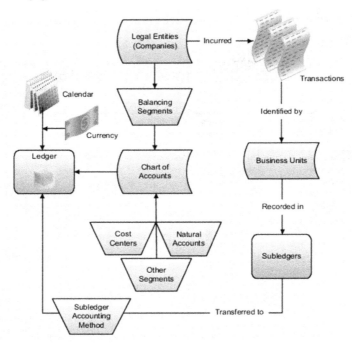

- ☐ As shown below ESC is a tool that guides you through the process of setting up a basic enterprise structure like a structure of divisions, legal entities, business units, and reference data sets that reflect the enterprise structure.
- ☐ Key Consideration when we use ECS
  - o start with your Financials requirements first before addressing your HCM requirements
  - o Do not utilize both ESC and Enterprise Structure Rapid Implementation Templates for the same configuration values
  - o ESC can only be used for the initial configuration and should not be used for configuration updates/maintenance.
  - o ERP objects like COA, Calendars, Ledgers, Cost Centers, Segment Values and Document sequences are not supported by the ESC

Rapid Implementation Templates

Another method of doing enterprise configuration is through Rapid Implementation. The rapid implementation task list minimizes the time needed for you to complete your key setups and enable the day-to-day use of Oracle fusion cloud

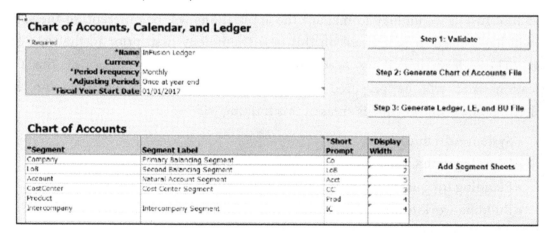

Sample Rapid implementation template

Key considerations for utilizing Rapid Implementation

- ☐ Primary Ledger is created for each unique country entered in the Companies and Legal Entities

- ☐ We cannot change the Chart of Accounts, Accounting Calendar, or Currency for your Ledgers after the setup is created
- ☐ We can create more than one hierarchy for any of your Chart of Account segments after the initial enterprise structure setup
- ☐ There is no rollback capability with Rapid Implementation Templates.

Data Conversion

Oracle ERP Cloud utilizes two methods for loading data

- ☐ ADF Desktop Integrator spreadsheet tool (ADFDI) - Use this MS Excel-based import feature to import small volumes of data that typically change on a periodic basis
- ☐ File-Based Data Import (FBDI) - Use the file-based data import feature to import large volumes of data from third-party or other Oracle applications

Both data loading tools do not have the ability to rollback transactional data once it has been committed to the cloud service environment.

User Training

As much of fusion technology to manage the applications will be different, so the support team will likely need to be trained on this new technology first, prior to the start of the project. These team members need to support the implementation of the Cloud Applications and will be prepared to support the applications once the project is completed. Some of the key focus areas of this training will be:

- ☐ • System Administration
- ☐ • Working with Oracle on provisioning and instance strategy
- ☐ • Planning for quarterly updates
- ☐ • Building workflow in BPEL
- ☐ • Data Conversion
- ☐ • Report development in OTBI
- ☐ • Administering workflow notifications
- ☐ • Configure screens and appearances

Adoption Choices for Existing EBS users

	2010	2011	2012	2013	2014	2015	2016	2017	2018	2019	2020	2021	2022	2023	2024	2025
11.5.10 GA Nov 2004	Nov 2010			Extended		Nov 2013	Exception	Dec 2015		Sustaining						
12.0 GA Jan 2007	Premier		Jan 2012		Extended		Jan 2016		Sustaining							
12.1 GA May 2009				Premier								Dec 2021		Sustaining		
12.2 GA Sep 2013				Sep 2013		Premier								Sep 2023	Sustaining	

Value Proposition for Customers on Release 12.2

Release 12.2.9 was delivered in 2019 and is the most recent update for 12.2. However, many Oracle E-Business Suite customers currently on Release 12.2.x are running 12.2.8. For 12.2.8 customers, the drivers to move to Oracle Cloud include the ability to:

☐ Evaluate new features of 12.2.9 and other releases.

☐ Upgrade to 12.2.9 on Oracle Cloud.

Optionally, migrate to Oracle Managed Cloud Service (OMCS) to run and maintain Release 12.2, for the following reasons:

☐ Release 12.2 online patching offers high availability but requires new technical skills.

☐ OMCS offers proven and efficient services for the ongoing use of online patching.

Continue on Your Current Path
- Upgrade to the latest release of your existing Oracle Applications portfolio

Adopt a Co-Existence Strategy
- Add new Fusion Applications modules or pillars to your existing Oracle Applications portfolio

Embrace the Complete Suite
- Deploy the comprehensive suite of Fusion Applications products

As illustrated above if you EBS is heavily customized and couldn't move to fusion immediately you have three choices

☐ Continue your current path by upgrading to latest12.2.X either in premise or cloud

☐ Adopt coexistence by implementing a few pillars in fusion and keep a few in EBS.

☐ Implement the complete Fusion cloud

Below are some of the Practical Paths to Cloud:

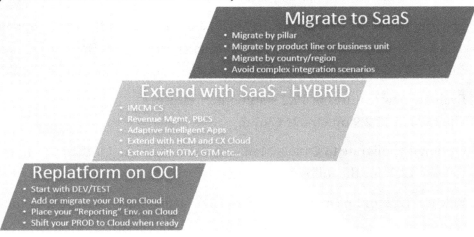

Practical Paths to Oracle Cloud for EBS Customers
Any Combination of these Paths – Journey to the Cloud

Migrate to SaaS
- Migrate by pillar
- Migrate by product line or business unit
- Migrate by country/region
- Avoid complex integration scenarios

Extend with SaaS - HYBRID
- IMCM CS
- Revenue Mgmt, PBCS
- Adaptive Intelligent Apps
- Extend with HCM and CX Cloud
- Extend with OTM, GTM etc...

Replatform on OCI
- Start with DEV/TEST
- Add or migrate your DR on Cloud
- Place your "Reporting" Env. on Cloud
- Shift your PROD to Cloud when ready

Below are some of the Practical Coexistence of EBS & Cloud Application which will give you a fair idea how Fusion customer world works at this moment

Oracle E-Business Suite and Practical Coexistence Scenarios
Extend with SaaS – Hybrid is the New Normal

E-Business Suite and HCM Cloud	E-Business Suite and ERP/SCM Cloud	E-Business Suite and CX Cloud

1. EBS HCM to Oracle Taleo Cloud Service
2. EBS HCM to Oracle Talent Management Cloud
3. EBS Payroll with Oracle HCM Cloud
4. EBS ERP to Oracle HCM Cloud
	Financials:
	  1. Revenue Management Cloud Service for EBS
	  2. Planning & Budgeting Cloud Service for EBS
	  3. Expense Cloud Service to EBS
	Projects:
	  4. Primavera Project Mgmt to EBS Projects
	  5. Project Portfolio Management Cloud to EBS
	Procurement:
	  6. Procurement /Sourcing Cloud for EBS
	  7. Procure-to-Pay Cloud to EBS (Indirect Proc)
	Logistics and Planning:
	  8. Supply Chain Planning Cloud for EBS
	  9. Transportation Management (OTM) Cloud to EBS
	  10. Global Trade Management (GTM) Cloud to EBS
	Manufacturing:
	  11. In-Memory Cost Management Cloud to EBS
	  12. PLM Cloud to EBS Item Master
		1. CPQ Cloud to EBS Order Fulfillment
		2. Sales Cloud with EBS Quoting
		3. Service Cloud (RightNow) to EBS Field Service
		4. Field Service Management (TOA) Cloud Service to EBS
		5. Order Management Cloud to EBS Order Fulfillment
		6. EBS ERP to Oracle CX Cloud

Fusion Application Adoption – Key Drivers and Benefits

- To reduce costs or streamline a critical business process - Fusion Financials eliminates costly, manual, & error-prone Financial Reconciliation & Disclosure Process with GL

- To rationalize information systems driven by a functional change in business - Fusion ERP for Global Financials & Sourcing Processes to eliminate separate instances in each country Oracle Fusion Applications Adoption

- To re-implement information systems driven by a technology change in business Line of Business Executives want to move a particular business process to Software-as-a-Service

- To eliminate a point solution and move more of their processes to Oracle - Fusion Human Capital offers Core Comply with global accounting standards and multiple legislative, industry, or geographic requirements

- Proactively resolve issues to expedite automated processing

- Improve decision making and increase accuracy during transaction entry

- Reduce transaction processing costs and data entry errors

- Utilize a cooperative system to work on, since the hardware, software, and processes are engineered to work together efficiently.

FINAL WORDS

EBS 12.X Promise: EBS 12.2.X releases promise to provide exiting technology and enhanced functionality. No urgency in moving to Fusion Cloud until Management and users like to adopt modern and cost-effective ERP

EBS Challenges: To Overcome EBS Challenges like Performance issues, Maintenance Cost, Period Close Burdens, In-house support cost can consider to Move to Fusion

Modern & Low-Cost ERP: EBS Finance, Procurement, HCM- Cloud Application can offer Modern ERP experience with lower cost

New Feature Adoption: EBS Order management, Projects, Manufacturing should start evaluating the adoption of new functionality and cost benefits of moving to the cloud

Cloud Method: Large Footprint-Phased Approach. Move specific process or specific country

Perception: Moving to Cloud is all about the change of business Perception- Losing Control over DB & Integrations, Standardizing the customization, Change Management adoption.

Technology: Integration/Reporting/Extension is Better tools; you need to know how to use them.

Evolving Product: Though Fusion is mature it is still evolving. Leverage the experience from early adopters.

Final Words: How business/Application is ready to go for Fusion Cloud. The migration to the cloud is inevitable, but the timing of this move is flexible.

ABOUT DOYENSYS

Doyensys, started in December 2006, is a rapidly growing Oracle technology-based solutions company located in the US with offshore delivery centers in India.

We specialize in Oracle e-Business Suite, Oracle Cloud, Oracle APEX Development, Oracle Fusion, Oracle Custom Development, Oracle Database, and Middleware Administration.

We provide business solutions using cutting-edge Oracle technologies to our customers all over the world. Doyensys uses a viable Global Delivery Model in deploying relevant and cost-effective solutions to its clients worldwide. A winning combination of technical excellence, process knowledge, and strong program management capabilities enables Doyensys achieve global competitiveness by making technology relevant to its customers.

We improve business efficiencies through innovative and best-in-class Oracle-based solutions with the help of our highly-equipped technical resources. We are an organization with a difference, which provides innovative solutions in the field of technology with Oracle products. Our clientele across the globe appreciate our laser focus on customer delight, which is our primary success parameter. We have more than 250 resources across the globe. The technical capability of Doyensys stands out from the crowd as we not only provide services of exceptional quality for various Oracle products on time but also take credit for having developed our own products such as DBFullview, EBIZFullview, DBIMPACT, SmartDB, etc.

Our customers are fully satisfied with our services and appreciate our work as we stretch beyond their expectations. We do not compromise on quality for delivery, and the policies of Doyensys revolve around PCITI [Passion, Commitment, Innovation, Teamwork, and Integrity].

Doyensys encourages its employees to participate in Oracle conferences across the globe, and our team has presented papers at various conferences such as AIOUG Sangam, OATUG Collaborate over the years.

The exemplary work of Doyens as a team has created a wonderful environment in the organization. The policies framed by the management are very flexible and employee-friendly, keeping in mind the growth and interest of the organization.

We received 'India's Great Mid-size Workplaces' award (Rank #19) based on the feedback given by our employees in strict confidence and evaluation of various parameters by Great Place to Work. We are an equal opportunity employer and do not discriminate based on sex, religion, gender, nationality, etc. Our women are given a lot of flexibility to work in the organization, understanding the time that they need to spend with their family.

We are also proud to share that we received the award 'Best Workplaces for Women' from Great Place to Work and were ranked among the top 75 in IT and BPM Best Workplaces.

The culture to excel is at the heart of everything Doyens do. We not only share and care for other folks within the organization but also for the folks around the globe.

We have Database and Oracle EBS blogs available on the Doyensys page and are accessible on the internet. These blogs are exemplary work done by Doyens from the knowledge and experience gained by supporting various customers across the globe. There is a habit of creating reusable components for the teams within Doyensys so that a similar piece of work can be helpful for some other project within the organization.

The management is very supportive and encouraging, which is very much visible from the awards [Passion and Commitment, Commitment and Customer Delight, Rookie of the Year] that are given to Doyens, who excel in various categories.

Doyensys is not only a great place to work but is also a great place to learn as employees are always encouraged to explore new technologies and suggest innovative ideas that can benefit the clients. The teams within Doyensys are always encouraged and recognized by the management to add value to the work that is delivered to the customer rather than just doing monotonous work.

ABOUT THE AUTHORS

ARCHANA RAGHU

Archana Raghu has 14+ years of overall IT experience in Oracle technologies involving various roles such as project management, technical and functional consulting, business process understanding, pre-sales activities, product development, etc.

She is a Certified Project Management Professional PMP® and a Certified Lean Six Sigma Black Belt. She is also a Certified Cloud Procurement 2017 Specialist with a strong background on Oracle Technologies like EBS, Fusion Applications, APEX, OBIEE, ADF, Web Services, and Mobile Apps. She does her best with the given opportunities to work on varied projects focusing on conceptualizing business needs and translating them into viable technical solutions. Her strengths include successful analysis and problem-solving expertise and proven project management experience.

She is a regular speaker at International Oracle Conferences such as OATUG Collaborate (Oracle Applications and Technology User Group) and AIOUG (All India Oracle User Group Conference) that are held in the US and India. She is best known for her presentation and training skills, and she always strives to keep herself updated on new technologies. She is currently working as a Project Manager at Doyen Systems Pvt. Ltd.

LinkedIn: https://www.linkedin.com/in/archana-raghu-4427381a/

SURYANARAYANA TVNS

Suryanarayana TVNS has more than eleven years of experience in Oracle technologies like EBS, Fusion Applications, OBIEE, Business Intelligence, BPM, ADF, Web Services, and Mobile Apps.

He is involved in various roles such as Senior Principal Consulting, Technical and Functional Consulting, and Business Process Understanding. Additionally, he also has important leadership qualities like decision-making skills, effective communication, motivation, and integrity.

He is an active participant in various Oracle seminars like OATUG, SANGAM, and recently presented for Collaborate 2019, which was held at San Antonio, Texas.

LinkedIn: https://www.linkedin.com/in/surya-narayana-753716116

PRATHAP NAGARAJAN

Prathap Nagarajan has eleven years of IT experience in Oracle Fusion Applications and Oracle e-Business Suite in Core HR, Payroll, and Absence Management Modules.

He is an Oracle Certified Professional who actively participates in AIOUG Oracle Conferences (All India Oracle User Group Conference). He is a great team leader and a quick learner who keeps himself updated with the new technologies.

He does his best to understand the business needs in upgrading them to the best practices in the Oracle Application. He is currently working as Senior Principal Consultant at Doyen Systems Pvt. Ltd.

LinkedIn: https://www.linkedin.com/in/prathap-nagarajan-732a6615/

ANANDKUMAR PALANISAMY

Anand Palanisamy has 8+ years of IT experience in Oracle technologies as a Technical Consultant.

He has strong experience in Oracle Fusion Application and Oracle e-Business Suite. He possesses additional knowledge of Oracle APEX, OBIEE, Web Services, JavaScript, XML, and Shell scripting.

He closely worked with foreign clients to understand their business needs and utilized his extensive problem-solving techniques to translate them into viable technical solutions.

He presented papers at International Oracle Conferences such as OATUG Collaborate (Oracle Applications and Technology User Group) and AIOUG (All India Oracle User Group Conference) that are held in the US and India.

He conducts training courses for peer technical developers and keeps himself abreast of the latest technologies.

He is currently working as a Senior Technical Consultant at Doyen Systems Pvt. Ltd.

LinkedIn: https://www.linkedin.com/in/anand-jp-00245237/

VIMAL MANIMOZHI

Vimal Manimozhi has been a Project Manager at Doyen Systems for around eight years. He has around fifteen years of experience in Oracle consulting, implementation, rollouts, upgrades, and product support of various applications, releases, and geographical locations. He has extensively worked in Finance, SCM, HRMS and Custom modules and has extensive experience in managing and delivering large projects.

He is an Oracle Cloud-certified Specialist with hands-on experience in implementing and supporting various cloud pillars like Finance, SCM, and Procurement and exposure to the latest technologies like Mobile App, EBS Automation, Blockchain and IoT.

He presented papers in various OAUG events across the globe, and he is the recipient of OAUG Star Presenter of the Year 2019.

LinkedIn: https://www.linkedin.com/in/vimalathithanm/

www.ingramcontent.com/pod-product-compliance
Lightning Source LLC
Chambersburg PA
CBHW080636060326
40690CB00021B/4961